notes from my kitchen table

notes from my kitchen table

DELICIOUS, EASY RECIPES
FOR HEALTHY, HAPPY LIVING

gwyneth paltrow

Foreword by Mario Batali
Photographs by Ellen Silverman

B⧫XTREE

First published 2011 by Boxtree
an imprint of Pan Macmillan,
a division of Macmillan Publishers Limited
Pan Macmillan, 20 New Wharf Road, London N1 9RR
Basingstoke and Oxford
Associated companies throughout the world
www.panmacmillan.com

ISBN 978-0-7522-2789-4

9 8 7 6 5 4 3 2 1

A CIP catalogue record for this book is
available from the British Library.

Photograph on page 10 © 2011 Frappe, Inc.
Family photographs on pages 13,14,15,16,21 and
257 appear courtesy of the Paltrow family.
Used by permission.
All other photographs © 2011 by Ellen
Silverman

Designed by Laura Palese
Illustrations by Danielle Deschenes

Printed and bound in Italy by Rotolito

Visit www.panmacmillan.com to read more about all
our books and to buy them. You will also find features,
author interviews and news of any author events,
and you can sign up for e-newsletters
so that you're always first to hear
about our new releases.

this book is dedicated to

my brother, Jake, my first guinea pig, who makes meals great just by being there, and for looking so much like Bruce while he is eating them. Also to our closest friends, our family really, who are always the reason to have a dinner party, the Wigmore-Reynolds, the Van Nices, the Carters, the Turly-Burnses and their extended clan, the Maudes, the Harveys, the Downeys, the McCartney-Willises, the Spielbergs, the Nadal-Saxe-Coburgs, the Conrad-Manions, the Hill-McGraws...

for Apple and Moses, hearts of my artichoke, my raisins d'être

author's note

I literally could not have written this book without the tireless, artful assistance of Julia Turshen, who stood over my shoulder at the stove and chopping block for the better part of a year, bringing a method to my freestyling madness. She quantified, tested and retested every recipe, oversaw the production of the photos, helped brainstorm in a crisis and, above all, was my intellectual and emotional support through the whole process.

contents

foreword

BY MARIO BATALI

In all great cultures on Terra Madre, food and family are deeply intertwined with tradition, pleasure and responsibility. Although it is only in the last couple of decades that Americans have awakened to the complexity and magnificence of our own gastronomic quilt – a pastiche of an infinite variety of cultures and delicious (relatively) young and modern gastronomic traditions – it has not dampened our intense fervour or our appetite for both the food and the history of our own families and heritage, even if cobbled together over a single generation. Although the Paltrows and the Batalis are relatively recent friends – of only twelve years – our approach to our family traditions is similarly sacred, and our intents and appreciations equal in both intensity and pleasure.

My family's historic events, major celebrations and even simple holidays have always been punctuated not only by food but by specific dishes. Christmas Eve at Grandma and Grandpa Batali's house was a series of traditional fish dishes, the same every year. Long before I knew or cared about the sacraments of the Catholic faith, I knew that the odd-smelling baccala and tomato sauce simmering on the back of the stove in Grandma's kitchen would be served with polenta and that crab would also be a part of our meal. That Grandma served the salad after the main course was always perceived as her forgetfulness, not her strategy and her family tradition from Abruzzo. When she dipped her biscotti into her wine after dinner, we thought she was nuts and laughed with her about the seemingly odd and wacky move.

Travelling with Gwyneth or sharing dinner with her at a restaurant or in our homes, I realized that her family's gastronomic traditions were as feverishly loved and observed as those in my family. Her passion for the delicious and her delightful and even obsessive curiosity went beyond simply eating good food. She also discovered and savoured its historical perspective and relevance. These are two of the reasons we decided to pursue our shared love of Spain in the TV series *Spain. . .On the Road Again.*

To eat with someone who loves food can double the fun. To eat with Gwyneth is even more than that. Let's put aside the fact that GP can effortlessly down a whole pan of perfect paella in Valencia or eat an entire plate of marinated anchovies in Barcelona. She simply loves not only the 'deliciousness' of each bite, but the fact that the ritual of the table is in itself a celebration. And when food, and its preparation, becomes so much more than mere nourishment, when it becomes entertainment and folly and libidinal pleasure all rolled into one thing? At that point every meal, every snack, every shared moment of sustenance can be a celebration. And it should be – not in a super serious way where overthinking can drain the fun from these moments, but in a carefree, sunrise-happy way.

Watching Gwyneth blossom as a mom cook has been fascinating. Her 'flexitarianism' has never been an issue in the family, and I do not think that her children think for a moment they are eating a 'special' way other than the fact that they know the shared meal itself is a special moment. They certainly do not eat 'fast' food or processed evil and will probably enjoy better health in the long run because of that. Either that or become junk food junkies in their rebellious teens as a result!

The fundamental generosity of cooking for others is a very special role for the mom who loves to cook and eat. The concept of nurturing is a learned one, and clearly GP's whole clan (actually, BOTH her natural family and her Spanish adopted family too!) shared this belief. If this book has been a delicious exercise of introspection and documentation for Gwyneth, then the creation of the website/blog GOOP.com has crystallized her point of view in the public domain. The intersection of the two is what we cooking enthusiasts can harvest as we think about and more importantly. . . ENJOY!

The most important thing to take from *Notes From My Kitchen Table* is the true pleasure we can derive from the thinking about, then the making of and finally the enjoyment of eating good food together with people we care about.

The best way to truly understand this book? Take the Perfect Roast Chinese Duck recipe (page 179) and follow the careful instructions to the T. Eat it with some people you love.

LIVE LARGE!

'To eat with someone who loves food can double the fun. To eat with Gwyneth is even more than that.'

introduction

Why? you may ask. In the last ten years or so, cooking has become my main ancillary passion in life. I have always loved food, being around it, preparing it, and of course eating it. This adoration was instilled in me by my incredible father, a supreme gourmand with a deep love for great food and wine.

I always feel closest to my father, who was the love of my life until his death in 2002, when I am in the kitchen. I can still hear him over my shoulder, heckling me, telling me to be careful with my knife, moaning with pleasure over a bite of something in the way only a Jew from Long Island can, his shoulders doing most of the talking. I will never forget how concentrated he looked in the kitchen, it almost looked like a grimace or a frown if you didn't know him. He practised incredible care and precision when he was preparing food. It was as if the deliciousness of the food would convey the love he felt in direct proportion.

He and I were always inseparable. When I was a baby, my mother was essentially the breadwinner in our house while my father was trying to rustle up a career in television. He walked me in his arms all night long as, by all accounts, I never slept. He took me everywhere with him, to each meeting and each diner, always ready to supply me with my fix of Red Cheek apple juice. We went to Jewish delicatessens and to now-extinct

drive-ins where I was introduced to the finer points of the egg cream and the ice cream float. Health food was never really on the agenda; it was about fun and deliciousness and togetherness.

When I was a kid in Santa Monica, California, he often took us out to eat in what was then the start of the 'California cuisine' era, taking great pride in my brother and me eating what would have been unheard of for him as a kid (oysters, artichokes, blue cheese, anything French). He looked forward to going out for a family meal with the genuine excitement of someone who never grew up eating in restaurants, and somehow that happiness, when we were all getting in the car, never seemed to wear off, no matter how many times we went to Michael's or 72 Market Street. For years, this excitement for food was limited to dining out – there wasn't a lot of agonizing over the home menu or tons of shopping and chopping. But that would change. Looking back, I think it all started with the pancakes.

My father was a master pancake maker. To the point that anyone who ever tried them would vouch that they were the best they had ever had. They still will to this day. They were thin, and light, and had that perfect subtle tang from fresh buttermilk. The pancake making started as a casual weekend breakfast thing and became a ritual. He became obsessed with perfecting them, eventually making the batter the night before as he was convinced it had some discreet effect on the outcome. Not only would we, his children and wife, delight in the taste of those mini stacks with warmed-up maple syrup, but our extended family of friends would as well, the size of the group often swelling to twenty or so. I think he started to feel the impact of making people so content and relaxed and sated with those pancakes. He was, after all, the most loving and nurturing of all men.

When I was about eighteen we started cooking together. I'm not sure exactly how it started, what day it was, or how it was catalysed. I just remember that we were both living back in Santa Monica (I was trying to get work as an actress and was hostessing in a fish restaurant) and we got tired of the giant supply of spaghetti and meatballs my mother had very kindly made and left in the freezer since she was working in New York. We decided to make a meal, and from there we got kind of obsessed. We would watch the cooking channel together as much as we watched NFL football, often with me resting in the crook of his arm. We would call each other with things we had learned, compare tips, recipes, and ideas like making salad dressing by putting all the ingredients into a little glass jar and shaking it up (utterly revolutionary to us at the time) or dicing an onion by cutting it in half vertically, making small slices vertically, then cutting horizontally, essentially eliminating the 'chopping'. 'What kind of moron am I that I nevah thought of this!' he would say in his heavily accented New York-ese.

My father's meals got more layered and more complex in lots of ways, and, in other ways, he stuck to his basic greatest hits. The most striking aspect of his cooking was how much joy he derived from feeding people that he loved. I mean, genuine, bursting happiness. And he instilled in me the idea that a meal made for your family is an expression of love, a source of pleasure – not only in the visceral enjoyment of the food, but also in the magic that is created when you imbue food with energy and nurturing.

I understood him more fully when I had my own children. Over the years I had learned how to cook through trial and error, through cooking classes, through lessons with chef friends, but it had always been for fun. Now it seemed much more, well, *important*. Unlike my daddy, who back in the day thought Oreos and a glass of milk were snack worthy, I became a bit obsessed with providing my kids with

healthy, unprocessed foods. This was informed by a period of eating a strictly macrobiotic diet, which, ironically enough, I had started when my father was diagnosed with throat cancer in the autumn of 1998. I was devastated by his diagnosis and became convinced that he could heal himself with good foods and alternative medicine, even if he was resistant to the (perhaps naive) idea. I armed myself by reading anything available that linked processed foods, pesticides, growth hormones, preservatives and the like to cancer and other diseases. I enlisted a macrobiotic counsellor who had healed herself from cancer by eating a 'healing diet' and also even brought on a chef to get us started. I was dealing with a man who upon hearing his cancer diagnosis went out for hot dogs and after an excruciating throat surgery wanted to go straight to Mr Chow. I think that he equated his beloved morning coffee with two sugars to being 'normal' and never embraced the idea of cutting anything out even if it would have made a difference in his health in the long run.

But all the information that I gathered did make a big personal impact. I learned about how the body can heal itself from almost anything. I learned about the physical and environmental effects of pesticides. I went strictly organic, local and macro and eliminated dairy, sugar, meat, alcohol, gluten, all (I think) in a bid to heal my father by proxy. Of course I couldn't cure him, but I found that my body felt really good. I loved eating this way and I stuck to it for years, although sometimes, damn, I just wanted a slice of coffee cake or a martini with olives.

When I was pregnant a few years later, I could not eat a bowl of brown rice for love or money. I wanted toasted cheese sandwiches and Baskin-Robbins Jamoca Almond Fudge ice cream, and, well, you can guess what won out. But when my daughter started eating solid food, the pendulum swung and again I focused on organic and whole foods. I did not want her to ingest pesticides, herbicides, growth hormones, antibiotics or preservatives and I still don't. In fact, sometimes I wonder if my father would still be alive today if he hadn't grown up eating so much of that stuff.

Through this process my father and daughter had unwittingly taught me the importance of balance. Could I use some butter and cheese and eggs in my cooking without going down some kind of hippie shame spiral? Yes. Of course I could. I would go back to eating chicken, but only once in a while and it would be free-range and organic. I would support my local farmers always, but if I needed some tomatoes in winter to slowly roast for soup, I would go to the supermarket.

This idea of balance became just an easing up on myself, which is something I find challenging to this day. On a broader scale, I try to remember this balance when I think about being a working mother. How do I cook for my family, do the school run, work on my projects, exercise, and not lose out on a great film project? I can't. And that's OK. Because my instincts have been shaped by a man who knew that family was everything. And my family will always be where I strive most for success. Making a home, cooking with love, and bringing everyone together are my tangible ways of achieving that kind of success.

My father, even through his deteriorating health in the aftermath of his cancer surgery, when his beloved red wine burned his throat and he struggled to chew and swallow, showed me through his own enjoyment that gathering round a table is the high point of the day. Through shared meals and meaningful togetherness, he made happiness feel achievable. He helped me realize it's all about the here and now, that happiness happens on a freezing winter night or in the garden when the weather's warm, often with a good bottle of wine, and always with the people you love. You just need some good ingredients and a few simple recipes, maybe a couple of jokes, or a 'topic to dissect' at the table, the way they do at Nora Ephron's house.

And there it is. It's what I believe in. In these pages you will find recipes for simple, (mostly) healthy, delicious food. This is the food I cook for my family and friends, over and over again, the food that never fails me. This book is meant to channel the ethos of my father by sharing the greatest gifts that he imparted to me. Invest in what's real. Clear up as you go. Drink while you cook. Make it fun. It doesn't have to be complicated. It will be what it will be.

why i don't eat red meat

I was raised a red-meat lover; I lived for brisket, ribs, meatballs, and especially Bolognese sauce. When I was twenty-one, a friend gave me a book called *Diet for a New America* by John Robbins, which exposed the brutal practices of American factory farms. Reading this book gave me a whole new perspective on what I was eating. That, coupled with a lecture I got from Leonardo DiCaprio (when he was nineteen and I was twenty-one) about how such animals are kept and processed, made me lose my desire for factory-farm pork and beef right there. I do, however, eat poultry. I always try to buy birds that are from farms where they are raised cage-free and organic. Chickens are victims of some of the worst factory-farming practices, so if it's not naturally raised, think twice.

Including my children in all aspects culinary is very important to me and always has been. When my daughter, Apple, was born in 2004, I always had her strapped to my chest in one of those BabyBjörn things and later on my hip in the kitchen while I stirred and chopped, one-handed at that!

Soon she was sitting up and I had fantasies of an extra-high high chair on wheels so she could be out of harm's way but privy to the action as I steamed and puréed her baby food. She was always trying to get a glimpse inside the pan, fascinated by the sounds of simmering and frying, or reaching to hold the big wooden spoon, mystified by its meaning (drumstick? teething device?).

Children are inherently curious about the process of cooking – it's mysterious and vaguely threatening, and seemingly for adults only. Fire and knives, no wonder my son is obsessed with it all. He, like my daughter, loves nothing more than helping me cook a meal. The trick is to let them participate as long as they are interested; eventually they wander off and busy themselves with something else, but lately they've been staying with it.

I believe it is the fact that I am carefully letting them do things that seem beyond their level that keeps them so interested. Whenever I am holding my son so that he can add salt to a sauce or stir something (with a long handle from a safe distance), I regularly think of some parenting advice my father gave on one occasion. His theory was that children positively respond to being trusted with something that they don't expect you to trust them with. And when they are trusted and complete something successfully, not only is their self-esteem buoyed but so is the connection between parent and child. Thus is my willingness to allow them to partake in some of the more adult tasks, with very careful supervision.

1. Turn the pepper grinder.
2. Add pinches of salt and
   other spices.
3. Stir batters and doughs
   in mixing bowls.
4. Spread butter on toast.
5. Grease cake tins.
6. Line muffin tins.
7. Crack eggs.
8. Whisk dressings.
9. Press the start button
   on appliances (with
   supervision, of course).
10. Add items to a blender,
    mixing bowl, etc.
11. Level off flour, sugar,
    etc.
12. Crush garlic in a press.
    (Watch their fingers!)

The three of us regularly engage in cooking together and doing this is one of my all-time favourite activities – all immersed in a project together, having fun and making dinner! It is a multitasker's dream, genuine quality time spent while checking something off the list.

It is my belief that children should know about food, should learn how to handle and prepare it. I think of it as a life skill no less important than any other. . . maybe more so as it will enable them to take control of their health as they get older. They have become well versed in their own likes and they often have opinions about how things are done.

Here are some of the ways that I include them in the process, ways you might be able to incorporate into your routine.

1. Go to the farmers' market or supermarket together. Give your children their own baskets and ask them to pick out vegetables or grains or fish that look interesting to them, anything that is fresh or dried, not processed. Look up recipes using the ingredients they have selected and have them choose something appealing to them. Easy books that focus on ingredient-driven, simple preparations are great (like *River Cafe Cookbook Easy*, by Rose Gray and Ruth Rogers, and Alice Waters's *The Art of Simple Food*, or look at epicurious.com or other foodie websites). If they are old enough, let them assist in the washing and preparing of the food. My kids beam with pride when they have had an impact on a family meal.

2. Make a kitchen garden. Go to your local nursery for young plants or peruse the Internet for seeds you can order. Kids love the process of watching things grow, especially when the choice of herb or vegetable was their idea. Plant veggies or herbs in a patch if you have a garden or even in pots by a sunny window or on a fire escape. Watering plants and checking their growth with a ruler is always fun. Get little veggie- and herb-picking baskets for them and let them do the cutting and picking themselves. (You will be surprised how well baby scissors work on a bunch of chives.)

3. Talk about the seasonality of the food, why and how things grow in different temperatures. Get a list of what grows when, starting with the season you are currently in. Narrow down the list to three or four of the fruits and vegetables in season and talk about appealing ways to cook

them. Go to local farms or join a co-op where you can pick what is growing. Do a bit of history on a food that is not native to your area and ask your kids to think about how it gets to your kitchen from where it has come from.

4. Make treats from scratch. Kids love carbs carbs carbs and so they should, they are delicious. In my kitchen we love to deep-fry French fries, so I make sure we do it often enough to satisfy cravings, but not every day or even every week. I always use organic vegetable oil and potatoes to try to convince myself that the French fries are healthy. Maybe not, but at least I know where the main ingredients are coming from. I try to alternate less-healthy cravings with healthy options as well: baked sweet potato fries still taste great with ketchup and are a much healthier alternative to deep-fried potatoes. Wholewheat pasta and brown rice are easily dressed up with a flavourful sauce. For sweet treats, the home-made version will always trump a shop-bought variety, which will always contain preservatives and other unsavoury ingredients. And always let the kids lick the bowl in reward for their concentration and hard work!

5. Expose your kids to the flavours of other countries and cultures. One fun way to do this is to ask your kids about what they think children are eating in a far-off land. Do some research about popular dishes and see what sounds interesting to them. Then make a menu plan and cook a meal with a theme from, for example, Mexico, Japan or Thailand – the options are endless – and you can try a different country every week. You can even listen to music from the country for extra inspiration.

6. Have your kids measure out ingredients. It's a great way to hone developing maths skills. If something calls for a cup of flour, I often hand my daughter a one-third-cup measuring cup and ask her how many of these she needs to put in the bowl to add up to one cup. You can make this as challenging or simple as suits your family.

how to use this book

To help you decide which recipes to make depending on your schedule and who you are cooking for, I've added icons to each recipe. Here is the key:

make-ahead

quick

vegetarian

vegan

one-pot meal

dress-up meal*

*a family-sized meal that can be tweaked during preparation/cooking/at the end to cater for both simpler and more sophisticated palates alike

There are also notes on some recipes: 'Make It Vegan' or 'Make It Kid Friendly' that offer you flexibility depending on your and your children's preferences.

Just to note that 1 tablespoon = 15ml in all recipes

trust yourself I am not a professional cook. I am an amateur and a lover of all things culinary. I learned to cook with trial and mostly error. Over the years I have learned three essential things: control your heat— watch the hob carefully, flavours are usually diminished by things cooking too quickly (though there are exceptions – trust yourself, and taste as you go. When you approach a meal with fear that it's going to be terrible, it probably will be. Approach it like it is going to be delicious. And don't forget the importance of the seasoning – that last pinch of salt or squeeze of lemon – especially when you're preparing simple, ingredient-driven food – can be the most important step.

the well-stocked
store cupboard

Oddly, some of the most exhilarating creative
moments I experience take place when I stand in the kitchen faced with the
task of making dinner when I wasn't expecting to. For the cook who comes
home from work and hasn't had time to go shopping, the importance of the
well-stocked store cupboard is paramount. The store cupboard for me isn't just
dried and canned goods. I make sure to have fresh things with a good shelf life
– garlic, onions, shallots, root vegetables, as well as home-made prepared items
I always keep in my fridge – Slow-Roasted Tomatoes (page 32), Basic Tomato
Sauce (page 30), along with celery, leeks and carrots, and herbs wrapped in
damp kitchen paper. With a well-stocked store cupboard, great meals can be
completely spontaneous.

OPPOSITE, FROM LEFT TO RIGHT: dark agave nectar, light agave nectar,
honeycomb, maple syrup, manuka honey, brown rice syrup

ESSENTIAL FOOD ITEMS
TO KEEP IN YOUR KITCHEN

Oils

Olive (I especially like extra virgin olive oil from Spain and Italy.)

Rapeseed (good for baking and dressings)

Safflower and groundnut (good for frying)

Grapeseed (great for dressings)

Toasted sesame and chilli sesame (good for flavouring)

Vinegars

Mostly I use red and white wine vinegar, but a variety, including balsamic, rice wine, sherry and champagne, is lovely to have on hand.

Condiments and Sauces

Vegenaise (My most often-used and beloved ingredient. It can be found at most grocery stores and all health food stores – unfortunately not yet in the UK. Regular mayo is fine and works, but Vegenaise is a healthier alternative.)

Dijon mustard

Coarse, seeded mustard

Tomato purée

Cholula hot sauce

Sriracha (Thai chilli sauce, commercial or home-made, see page 35)

Miso (white, barley and red)

Unsweetened peanut butter

Good jams and conserves (including ginger, raspberry, blueberry and apricot)

Real Vermont maple syrup

Mirin

Fish sauce

Soy sauce

Bragg Liquid Aminos

Canned Goods

Canned tuna (packed in olive oil)

Anchovies

Beans (including kidney, black, cannellini and butter beans)

Canned whole peeled tomatoes with their juice

Rices, Pastas, Pulses

Dried lentils

Pastas (including spaghetti, penne, pappardelle, rigatoni, macaroni and wholewheat pasta)

Soba noodles

Short-grain brown rice

Bomba rice (for paella)

Go-To Produce

Onions (yellow and red)

Garlic

Fresh ginger

Lemons

Celery

Carrots

Herbs (including basil, parsley, coriander and chives)

In the Fridge

Organic butter

Organic large eggs

Bacon (I use a lot of turkey and duck bacon.)

Cheese (including Parmigiano-Reggiano and other hard cheeses that will last the longest if wrapped properly in an airtight container or clingfilm, also Gorgonzola, mozzarella – which lasts only for two to three days – and mature Cheddar)

In the Freezer

Stocks
Vegetable Stock (page 36)
Fish Stock (page 40)
Chicken Stock (page 39)

Ice cream

Frozen vegetables (including peas, sweetcorn and edamame/soya beans)

For Baking

Arrowroot or cornflour

Bicarbonate of soda

Baking powder

Light agave nectar

Brown rice syrup

Flours (including white spelt, whole spelt, buckwheat and unbleached plain)

Sugars (including unrefined dark brown, icing and granulated cane)

Vanilla pods and/or extract

The Spice Shelf

Maldon salt

Coarse additive-free or kosher salt

Garam masala

Celery seeds

Cinnamon (whole and ground)

Cumin (whole and ground)

Chilli powder

Crushed chillies

Fennel seeds

Coriander seeds

Nutmeg

Black peppercorns

Pimenton (Spanish smoked paprika)

Dried whole chillies

Saffron

Cloves (whole and ground)

Ground ginger

Wasabi powder

Some Other Ingredients

Bonito flakes, kombu, wakame and kimchi (found in Asian grocery shops or online – see page 266)

Salt-packed capers

Strong bread flour or 00 flour (both the higher-protein 'bread' and 'pasta' varieties for pizza and pasta doughs – found in Italian delicatessens or online)

Nuts (including almonds, walnuts and pecans)

Seeds (including sunflower, pumpkin and sesame)

Dried fruit (including raisins and cranberries)

RECIPES FOR STOCKS, SAUCES & SPECIAL INGREDIENTS

basic tomato sauce

THIS SAUCE IS A SIMPLE, perfect tomato sauce. Slow cooked to bring out the sweetness, it is the perfect base for many things in this book and delicious on its own with some penne or spaghetti. My daughter eats this maybe slightly too often . . . my son prefers pesto.

2 tablespoons extra virgin olive oil

6 cloves garlic, peeled and thinly sliced

4 fresh large basil leaves

4 400g cans whole peeled tomatoes with their juice

Coarse salt

Freshly ground black pepper

Heat the olive oil in a large saucepan over low heat, add the garlic and cook for 5 minutes. Add 2 of the basil leaves and stir for a minute. Add the tomatoes and their juice and the 2 remaining basil leaves. Turn the heat to high. Bring the sauce to the boil, turn the heat to low, season with salt and pepper, and let it bubble away on low heat for 45 minutes, stirring occasionally and crushing the tomatoes with your wooden spoon. Cool and refrigerate.

 YIELD: 1 litre · ACTIVE PREPARATION TIME: 15 minutes
TOTAL PREPARATION TIME: 1 hour

roasted peppers

ROASTED RED PEPPERS WERE AMONG the first antipasti my father learned to prepare (and with great pride). In his version, after roasting, sweating and peeling the peppers, he would marinate them in olive oil and (painfully) thinly sliced garlic overnight. The next day he would bring them back to room temperature, lay some anchovies over the top, and finish with a scattering of coarsely chopped flat-leaf parsley. He would serve them with a massive smile on his face, like he really had gotten this gourmet thing down. They are great to have on hand to serve up à la Bruce, in a roast veggie sandwich or panini, or to top a salad niçoise.

Roast whole peppers over an open gas flame on high heat, rotating with tongs, until completely blackened all over. Be patient – you want the flesh to soften and the skin to be totally, totally charred; it should take 15 or 20 minutes. After the peppers are cooked, put them in a large metal or glass bowl, cover it with clingfilm, and let them sit until they're cool enough to handle (the covered bowl creates steam which makes it super easy to peel the peppers). Incidentally, a plastic bag works too.

When they're cool, slip off and discard the charred skins, running them under water as needed to remove all the skin. Cut the peppers open and discard the seeds. These keep for 1–2 weeks well rubbed with a little olive oil and stored in an airtight container in the refrigerator.

 YIELD: flexible • ACTIVE PREPARATION TIME: ½ hour • TOTAL PREPARATION TIME: 1 hour

vanilla sugar

SWEET RECIPES ALWAYS BENEFIT from using real vanilla pods, their beautiful paste scraped out, adding those delightful black flecks to batter, French toast, anything your heart desires. Instead of throwing the empty pods in the bin or compost, I add them to a jar of organic sugar, which is then infused with the vanilla flavour, nice when baking.

slow-roasted tomatoes

A STORE CUPBOARD ESSENTIAL. THIS METHOD turns even the most flavourless out-of-season winter tomatoes into gorgeous, sweet ones. I always have them in the fridge to brighten up sandwiches, salads, cheese plates and the like.

Vine-ripened tomatoes

Olive oil

Salt

Preheat the oven to 140°C (275°F) gas 1.

Cut the tomatoes in half horizontally, rub with a tiny bit of olive oil and a pinch of salt and bake seed side up in the preheated oven for 3–5 hours, or until they look nearly sun dried (the edges will be caramelized and the moisture will be almost entirely evaporated). These keep, well refrigerated in an airtight container with a bit of olive oil, for at least a week, so make a whole bunch at once.

YIELD: flexible · ACTIVE PREPARATION TIME: 5 minutes
TOTAL PREPARATION TIME: 3–5 hours

'I'm not gluten free but I like gluten-free food.'

—APPLE

lee's home-made sriracha

LEE GROSS IS A (MOSTLY) MACROBIOTIC chef I have known and worked with at various times over the past decade. He was the chef who taught me about macrobiotics around the time that my father became ill and I got hell bent on the family eating better. Trained by Michio Kushi at the Kushi Institute in Becket, Massachusetts, and at Johnson & Wales in Rhode Island, Lee beautifully fuses the concepts of healthy and delicious. He has taught me a world of food knowledge that I apply all the time. One day when I was talking about my love for this spicy, smoky condiment, he informed me that it was full of chemicals. Luckily he came up with this version, which is just as delicious and preservative free! Don't worry – it still keeps for ages in the fridge.

170g	garlic cloves, peeled (about 2 heads)
450g	red jalapeño chillies, stemmed and sliced into thin rings (remove some seeds for a milder sauce)
550ml	rice wine vinegar
75ml	light agave nectar
2	tablespoons coarse salt
1	tablespoon ground arrowroot
2	tablespoons fish sauce (or you can substitute soy sauce if you are vegetarian)

Put the garlic in a small saucepan and add cold water just to cover. Bring to the boil, immediately drain, cool the garlic under running water, and return it to the saucepan. Cover with cold water and repeat the blanching process. Thinly slice the blanched garlic and combine with the chillies and vinegar in a larger pan. Bring to the boil, cook for 3 minutes and remove from the heat. Add the agave and salt and stir to combine. Let mixture sit undisturbed for 1 hour to steep and cool.

Whizz the mixture in a blender until smooth (it's OK if all the seeds don't blend in). Return the puréed sauce to the pan, bring to the boil, lower the heat and simmer for 10–15 minutes, skimming any foam as necessary, until the sauce is slightly reduced and has some body.

In a small bowl, dissolve the arrowroot with 1 tablespoon of lukewarm water. Whisk into the simmering sauce and cook for 2 minutes more, or until the sauce is nicely thickened (it should be slightly thinner than ketchup). Remove the sauce from the heat, let cool slightly and stir in the fish sauce.

 YIELD: 1.2 litres • **ACTIVE PREPARATION TIME:** 30 minutes • **TOTAL PREPARATION TIME:** 2 hours

vegetable stock

GOOD STOCK IS ESSENTIAL to have in your freezer. As vegetable stock out of a carton can be completely insipid, I started making and freezing this robust stock since it brings vegetarian soups and stuffings up a notch.

1 large onion, peeled and roughly chopped

2 large carrots, peeled and roughly chopped

1 stalk celery, roughly chopped

1 large leek, roughly chopped

3 cloves garlic, peeled and whacked with the back of your knife

4 sprigs fresh parsley

4 sprigs fresh thyme

2 sprigs fresh tarragon

1 bay leaf

1 teaspoon coarse salt

1 teaspoon black peppercorns

3l cold water

Combine everything in a saucepan. Bring to the boil, lower the heat and simmer for 45 minutes. Let it cool and strain into a clean container. Keeps 1–2 weeks in the fridge, 6 months in the freezer.

YIELD: 3 litres · ACTIVE PREPARATION TIME: 10 minutes
TOTAL PREPARATION TIME: 1 hour plus cooling

chicken stock

THIS STRAIGHTFORWARD CHICKEN STOCK is foolproof and makes a great base. Be sure to use organic chicken!

1 organic whole chicken, washed and dried (See Salt Scrubs for Poultry, page 43.)

1 teaspoon black peppercorns

1 bay leaf

2 stalks celery, roughly chopped

1 large onion, peeled and roughly chopped

2 carrots, peeled and roughly chopped

3 sprigs fresh parsley

3 sprigs fresh thyme

1 teaspoon coarse salt

Put all of the ingredients into a large soup pot, cover with cold water (should take about 3 litres), and bring to the boil over high heat. Skim any foam that rises to the top, turn the heat down to low and simmer for 1½ hours. Let the stock cool and then strain into containers to freeze. The chicken makes for great chicken salad or you can shred it into the strained broth, add a couple of carrots cut into coins and some diced celery, and enjoy some delicious soup.

Keeps 1–2 weeks in the fridge, 6 months in the freezer.

 YIELD: about 2.5 litres • **ACTIVE PREPARATION TIME:** 10 minutes
TOTAL PREPARATION TIME: 2 hours plus cooling

fish stock

FISH STOCK IS ESSENTIAL for paella, fish soups and risottos. Make a large quantity and freeze it. As with other stocks, it really comes in handy – especially if you are cooking last minute.

Shells from 4 lobsters or shells and heads of 6 prawns (I keep them in a plastic bag in the freezer after a special dinner.)

Bones from 1 halibut (or any other bones from not-too-oily fish; ask your fishmonger – he should be happy to give them to you)

2 stalks celery, roughly chopped

1 onion, peeled and roughly chopped

1 large leek, thoroughly cleaned and roughly chopped

3 carrots, peeled and roughly chopped

2 bay leaves

3 sprigs fresh parsley

1 tablespoon peppercorns

1 tablespoon coarse salt or Maldon sea salt

Combine everything in a large saucepan and cover with cold water. Bring to the boil, skim any foam that rises to the surface, lower the heat and simmer for 25–30 minutes. Let the stock cool and then strain it into containers for the freezer or use it immediately for a soup or a paella.

Keeps 1–2 weeks in the fridge, 6 months in the freezer.

YIELD: about 5 litres · ACTIVE PREPARATION TIME: 10 minutes
TOTAL PREPARATION TIME: 40 minutes plus cooling

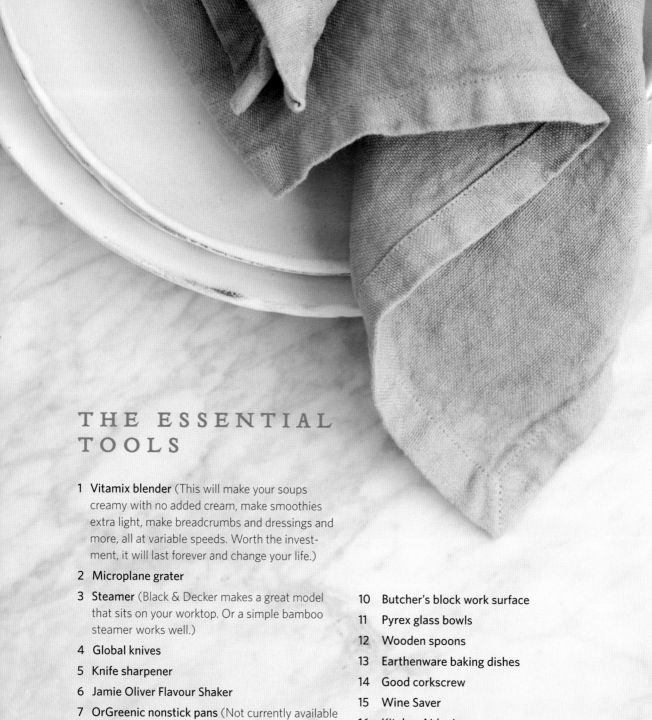

THE ESSENTIAL TOOLS

1 **Vitamix blender** (This will make your soups creamy with no added cream, make smoothies extra light, make breadcrumbs and dressings and more, all at variable speeds. Worth the investment, it will last forever and change your life.)

2 **Microplane grater**

3 **Steamer** (Black & Decker makes a great model that sits on your worktop. Or a simple bamboo steamer works well.)

4 **Global knives**

5 **Knife sharpener**

6 **Jamie Oliver Flavour Shaker**

7 **OrGreenic nonstick pans** (Not currently available in the UK)

8 **Le Creuset cast-iron casserole**

9 **Stainless steel cookware** (All-Clad is my favourite.)

10 **Butcher's block work surface**

11 **Pyrex glass bowls**

12 **Wooden spoons**

13 **Earthenware baking dishes**

14 **Good corkscrew**

15 **Wine Saver**

16 **KitchenAid mixer**

17 **KitchenAid pasta roller attachment**

18 **Cheap stainless steel bowls**

19 **Baking trays**

PREPPING TECHNIQUES FOR POULTRY & CLAMS

salt scrubs for poultry

Before I cook a chicken or a duck, I always wash it carefully. First I wet it with cold water and then I scrub it with a handful of coarse kosher or rock salt. Then I rinse it with more water and pat it completely dry, inside and out, with kitchen paper. My grandmother Dorothy (my father's mother) called it 'koshering' a chicken, although I'm not sure it's possible to do that after the fact . . .

salt scrubs for clams

I once learned a great way to clean clams. First you fill a bowl with cold water and let the clams soak for about 10 minutes. Then drain them, sprinkle them with a handful of coarse salt and scrub them against themselves, picking them up by the handful and rubbing them together. Do this hard enough to get any and all dirt off, but with a soft enough touch so as not to break the shells. Rinse the clams, soak them in cold water again and then drain them when the pan is ready for them.

IF YOU HAVEN'T HAD TIME TO GO TO THE HEALTH FOOD OR GOURMET STORE...

Your body will thank you if you make the upgrade.

IF YOU DON'T HAVE...	YOU CAN USE...	WHY BOTHER...
Spelt flour (white or whole)	Equal parts unbleached plain flour OR wholemeal flour	Although spelt contains gluten, it's easier to digest than regular wheat flour and is less taxing on the system.
Barley flour	Equal parts unbleached plain flour OR wholemeal flour	Barley flour is derived from barley – which contains each of eight essential amino acids. It's much better than white flour at regulating blood sugar.
Buckwheat flour	Equal parts unbleached plain flour OR wholemeal flour	Buckwheat also contains eight essential amino acids and is a bit of a super food – rich in copper, iron, B vitamins, magnesium, phosphorus, zinc and flavonoids. It lowers cholesterol, blood pressure and glucose levels, is high in fibre, and doesn't have gluten.
Raw unrefined dark brown sugar	Dark brown sugar	Unrefined sugar is made directly from sugar cane and is an unprocessed product and has antioxidants. Normal supermarket brown sugar is actually just white processed sugar with molasses stirred in for colour and flavour.
Grade B real Vermont maple syrup	3 parts honey plus 1 part water OR 225g white sugar for every 180ml maple syrup	Low on the glycaemic index, a great source of manganese and zinc, maple syrup is one of North America's great ingredients. It's always in my kitchen.
Light agave nectar	Equal parts brown rice syrup OR 3 parts honey plus 1 part water	Agave is super low on the glycaemic index and has lots of minerals including potassium, magnesium, iron and calcium.
Soya milk, rice milk, almond milk, hemp milk	Cow's milk	Alternative milks have a variety of health benefits – especially for the lactose intolerant. Rice milk, almond milk and hemp milk specifically are full of nutrients and are easy to digest.
Turkey, duck and/ or tempeh bacon	Pork bacon	If you aren't into animals of the four-legged variety, but still adore the taste and smell of bacon, it's great to have another option. D'Artagnan duck bacon, if available, is out of this world.
Vegenaise	Hellmann's mayonnaise	Vegenaise is one of my favourite things on the planet – you would never know it's not real mayonnaise and you are forgoing all of the cholesterol. I'm not vegan, but I prefer it over mayonnaise every day of the week.

soups

The stove is really the epicentre of my house –
I am never far from it and most of the time there is something on top of
it, simmering away for my family. I am constantly thinking about ways to
give my children dishes filled with as much nutritional value as possible
and that's where soup is a real hero. Hearty or light, creamy or chunky, hot
or chilled, soup often offers the best ways to use seasonal, local ingredients
– the options are never-ending. In this chapter you will find nourishing,
simple, healthy ways to turn that trip to the farmers' market into a surefire
way to get kids to eat the bounty that is offered there. (My son may not be
totally convinced on this front, but we'll get there . . .)

butternut squash soup

ONE COLD WINTER EVENING I dreamed up this velvety squash soup.
The garam masala brings a sweet spice that really complements the flavour of
the squash. Lovely as a first course with Indian-Spiced Tuna Steaks (page 150)
or in little bowls as an after-school warm-up.

1 tablespoon extra virgin
olive oil

2 tablespoons unsalted
butter

2 large onions, peeled and
roughly chopped

2 cloves garlic, peeled and
finely chopped

1 teaspoon coarse salt

½ teaspoon freshly ground
black pepper

½ teaspoon garam masala
or your favourite curry
powder

1 large butternut squash,
peeled, seeded and diced

1l Vegetable Stock (page
36), warmed

Heat the olive oil and butter in a soup pot over medium heat. Add the onion
and garlic and sauté for about 10 minutes, or until beginning to soften. Add
the salt, pepper and garam masala and cook for another 2 minutes. Add the
squash and cook for another 10 minutes, stirring occasionally. Pour the stock
into the pot – if it doesn't quite cover the squash, add some boiling water.
Bring to the boil, lower to a simmer and cook until the squash is very tender,
about 20 minutes.

Let it cool for at least 15 minutes and then purée it in batches in a
blender. Be very careful when blending hot liquids. Start slowly and work
in batches if necessary (you don't want the steam to blow the lid off). Pour
back into the pot, gently heat, season with salt and serve.

SERVES: 4 · ACTIVE PREPARATION TIME: ½ hour
TOTAL PREPARATION TIME: 1 hour plus 10 minutes

vegetarian chilli

THIS MEAL WAS ONE of the first I devised especially for my children.
My daughter is completely vegetarian (she came to this entirely on her own),
so protein from beans and other veggie sources are a big part of her life (and
therefore mine). I love this chilli because apart from the fact that it contains
three different types of beans, it easily becomes one of those 'dress-up' meals as
I call them – a slight adjustment and they transition simply from tasting good
to a kid's palate to pleasing an adult's. My kids like this chilli with rice, and
we grown-ups top it off with a tablespoon of crème fraîche (or yogurt), some
chopped spring onions and coriander, and a dash of hot sauce.

2 tablespoons extra virgin olive oil

½ large onion, peeled and finely diced

1 large carrot, peeled and cut into 5mm dice

½ large red pepper, seeds and ribs removed, cut into 5mm dice

2 cloves garlic, peeled and finely chopped

¾ teaspoon mild chilli powder

½ teaspoon ground cumin

¼ teaspoon freshly ground black pepper

1 teaspoon chipotle chillies in adobo sauce

2 400g cans whole peeled tomatoes with their juice

100g Puy lentils (small, dark French lentils that hold their shape well), rinsed and drained

1 410g can black beans, rinsed and drained

1 410g can kidney beans, rinsed and drained

Big pinch coarse salt

3 tablespoons tomato purée

Heat the olive oil in a large saucepan over medium heat. Add the onion, carrot, red pepper, garlic, chilli powder, cumin and black pepper. Cook, stirring, for 15 minutes, or until the vegetables are softened. Add the chipotle and stir to combine.

Turn the heat up to high, add the tomatoes and their juice, crushing them a bit with your wooden spoon, and bring to the boil. Reduce the heat to low and simmer for 40 minutes.

Add the lentils and beans. Fill one 410g can with water and add it to the pan, along with the salt. Bring to the boil, lower the heat and simmer for 40 minutes.

Stir in the tomato purée and cook for 20 more minutes, or until the lentils are soft and the flavours are melded.

let the kids help   This is great to make at the weekend when you may have some extra time. My kids love to participate in the process by rinsing and adding the various kinds of beans, measuring out the spices and stirring the pan. It keeps in the fridge all week and is great for a super casual dinner or an after-school bite.

SERVES: 4 • ACTIVE PREPARATION TIME: ½ hour
TOTAL PREPARATION TIME: 2 hours

best miso soup

DURING THE STRICT MACROBIOTIC CHAPTER of my life, I ate miso soup every day for breakfast and sometimes with dinner as well. It became one of my real comfort foods. Since it's full of minerals and said to counter radiation and free radicals in the body, I always feel happy when my kids are slurping it out of those giant ceramic spoons. I use white miso when I'm in the mood for a lighter, sweeter version or barley miso when I'm looking for that depth of flavour.

1.5l	water (filtered is best)
50g	dried bonito flakes
3	dried shiitake mushrooms
1	10cm piece dried wakame seaweed
100ml	miso paste
75g	watercress leaves, washed (optional)

Heat the water in a large saucepan and when bubbles form around the edges, add the bonito. Turn the heat down and simmer for 2 minutes.

Turn off the heat and let the broth sit for 5 minutes. Strain the broth into a clean pan, discarding the bonito. Add the shiitakes and wakame to the broth and simmer over low heat for 20 minutes.

Remove the wakame and mushrooms. Discard the thick stems from the mushrooms, thinly slice the caps and slip them back into the soup. Chop the wakame into small pieces, discarding any thick pieces of stem, and return to the pan.

In a small bowl, combine the miso paste with a bit of the broth and whisk to combine. Pour the mixture back into the pan and let the soup simmer, being careful not to let it boil. If you're using it, add the watercress at the last minute just to wilt it, and serve.

SERVES: 4 • ACTIVE PREPARATION TIME: 10 minutes • TOTAL PREPARATION TIME: ½ hour

You can make the dashi – the bonito, shiitake and wakame broth – in advance and then add the miso whenever you're ready to eat.

tortilla soup

I FELL IN LOVE with tortilla soup (and all things Tex-Mex) when I was
doing a movie called *Flesh and Bone* in Austin, Texas, in 1992 (I was nineteen).
As I had a small part in the film, I had a lot of time to discover the wonders
of Texan cuisine – huevos rancheros, BBQ brisket – and to firmly fall in love
with chillies of every variety. Tortilla soup became the thing I ate the most, a
teenager in a hotel room, feeling very comforted by the texture and big flavour
of this spicy, hearty soup. It's usually made with chicken but I sought to make
a vegetarian version for my daughter and it worked beautifully.

2l	Vegetable Stock (page 36) or prepared low-sodium vegetable stock
1	bunch fresh coriander, stems and leaves separated
2	dried medium-sized whole red chillies (preferably New Mexican *guajillo* or cascabel chillies)
5	cloves peeled garlic, 2 crushed and 3 finely chopped
60ml	plus 1 tablespoon vegetable oil
1	onion, peeled and diced
1	400g can whole peeled tomatoes with their juice
	Large pinch coarse salt
¼	teaspoon freshly ground black pepper
1	avocado, peeled, stoned and diced
2	spring onions, finely sliced
	Juice of ½ lime
4	good-quality corn tortillas

Heat the vegetable stock over a very low heat in a soup pot with the
coriander stems, one of the chillies, and the crushed garlic.

Meanwhile, toast the other chilli over an open flame just until it starts
to get fragrant. Roughly chop it, discarding the stem and seeds, and reserve.
Heat the 1 tablespoon of vegetable oil over medium-high heat in a medium
frying pan. Add the onion, chopped garlic and reserved chopped chilli. Sauté
for about 5 minutes, or until the onion starts to pick up a little colour. Add the
tomatoes and their juice, salt and pepper, turn the heat down very low and
let the mixture cook for 40 minutes, or until nearly all of the moisture has
evaporated. Stir it occasionally, breaking the tomatoes up a bit as you go.

In a blender, whizz the tomato mixture with a ladleful of stock until
smooth. Remove the coriander stems, chilli and garlic from the stock and add
the blended tomatoes. Stir to combine and then cook over the lowest heat
possible for an hour to really let the flavours get to know each other. Season
with salt and pepper if necessary.

When you're ready to eat, roughly chop 2 tablespoons of the coriander
leaves and toss with the avocado and spring onions in a small bowl and
squeeze the lime over the mixture. Cut the tortillas into 1cm-thick strips.
Heat the 60ml of vegetable oil over medium-high heat in a frying pan and
fry the tortillas for about 1½ minutes, or until lightly browned and crisp.
Drain the tortilla strips on kitchen paper.

Ladle the soup into four bowls and distribute the tortillas and avocado
mixture on top of each. As you eat, dip the tortillas into the soup, letting
them soften, and be sure to get a bit of avocado in each bite.

SERVES: 4 • ACTIVE PREPARATION TIME: ½ hour
TOTAL PREPARATION TIME: 1 hour plus 10 minutes

duck broth with soba

THERE USED TO BE A PLACE on Mercer Street in New York's SoHo called Honmura An. It was a completely unique restaurant in Manhattan at the time, one that introduced me to the virtues of home-made, hand-made soba noodles. Whenever I would come home from some far-flung movie location, I would head straight there. It closed when the owner moved back to Japan, leaving us soba lovers lost and forlorn. I haven't learned how to make home-made soba noodles yet, but the organic packaged variety are pretty great and as they are made with buckwheat flour, they are a healthier choice than a white flour noodle. I make this the day after I make the Perfect Roast Chinese Duck and think about Koichi, the restaurant's welcoming owner.

1	duck carcass (best to make this soup after you make Perfect Roast Chinese Duck, page 179)
3	star anise
1	cinnamon stick
3	cloves
1	teaspoon black peppercorns
1	bunch fresh coriander
5	cloves garlic, peeled and crushed
1	5cm piece ginger, peeled and crushed
1	onion, peeled and roughly chopped
225g	buckwheat soba noodles
80–120ml	barley miso
4	tablespoons thinly sliced spring onions
4	tablespoons coarsely chopped fresh coriander leaves
1	small bunch enoki mushrooms or beansprouts (optional)

In a large stockpot, combine the duck carcass with the star anise, cinnamon, cloves, peppercorns, coriander stems, garlic, ginger and onion. Cover with cold water (it should take about 2 litres), bring to the boil and lower the heat, skimming off any foam that accumulates. Simmer over a low heat for at least 1 hour, up to 2. Strain the broth into a clean pan and keep it warm while you prepare the soba noodles.

Cook the soba noodles according to the packet directions, keeping them on the al dente side. When they're cooked, rinse them immediately with cold water to keep them from getting soggy. Meanwhile, whisk 80ml of the miso with a ladleful of broth in a small bowl and return the mixture to the broth. Taste and repeat with more miso if needed, remembering it's easier to add more than to take it out.

To serve, distribute the soba noodles into four soup bowls. Ladle the broth over them and sprinkle each serving with a tablespoon each of spring onions and coriander and a few enoki mushrooms.

make it kid friendly   Once the soba is cooked and rinsed it can be stir-fried with some garlic and Braggs Liquid Aminos or soy sauce for the kids. Add veggies and tofu if liked.

 SERVES: 4 · ACTIVE PREPARATION TIME: 20 minutes · TOTAL PREPARATION TIME: 1½ hours

broccoli & cheese soup

LUCKILY, MY CHILDREN LOVE BROCCOLI, and although we sometimes enter into UN-like negotiations about how many 'trees' they need to eat before they can partake of ice cream, it is a vegetable that they tend to embrace. When I want to give it a new look, this soup does just the trick. I like to add a nice strong Stilton to mine (my love for strong cheese is well known and well feared in my house) and my kids love it with Cheddar. You can determine how mature or mild you want it. Any way you serve it up, it hits the spot.

2	tablespoons extra virgin olive oil
2	cloves garlic, peeled and thinly sliced
1	onion, peeled and roughly diced
2	large stalks broccoli (about 600g), cut into small florets
1l	Vegetable Stock (page 36), Chicken Stock (page 39) or water
½	teaspoon coarse salt
¼	teaspoon freshly ground black pepper, plus more for serving
40g	rocket (watercress would be good too)
30–60g	crumbled, strong, assertive Stilton for the adults or grated mature Cheddar for the kids
	Your best, highest-quality olive oil, for serving

Heat the olive oil in a large saucepan over medium heat. Add the garlic and onion and sauté for just a minute, or until fragrant. Add the broccoli and cook for 4 minutes, or until bright green. Add the stock, salt and pepper, bring to the boil, lower the heat and cover. Cook for 8 minutes, or until the broccoli is just tender. Pour the soup into a blender and purée with the rocket until quite smooth. Be very careful when blending hot liquids. Start slowly and work in batches if necessary. Pour the soup back into the pan, stir in 30g of the cheese, taste, and add more if you'd like. Serve with extra black pepper and a drizzle of your best olive oil.

SERVES: 4 • ACTIVE PREPARATION TIME: 15 minutes • TOTAL PREPARATION TIME: ½ hour

You can freeze it without the cheese.

cold pea & basil soup

THIS EASY, VELVETY PEA SOUP is bright green and cool, perfect for
a summer's eve. You can gently heat it as well; kids seem to like it
warmed through.

2	tablespoons extra virgin olive oil
2	small or 1 large onion, peeled and finely diced
600g	frozen peas
1l	Vegetable Stock (page 36)
12	fresh large basil leaves, 10 whole, 2 finely sliced for serving
	Coarse salt
	Freshly ground black pepper
	Sour cream or your best, highest-quality olive oil, for serving

Heat the olive oil in a large saucepan over medium heat, add the onion and
cook until soft, about 10 minutes. Add the peas and stock, bring to the boil,
lower the heat and simmer for 10 minutes. Remove from the heat and add
the whole basil leaves and salt and pepper to taste. Let the soup cool and
then whizz in a blender until smooth. Cool in the refrigerator for at least
2 hours.

Serve garnished with a spoonful of sour cream and the finely sliced basil.

SERVES: 4 • ACTIVE PREPARATION TIME: 25 minutes
TOTAL PREPARATION TIME: 25 minutes plus at least 2 hours cooling

slow-roasted tomato soup: two ways

WHEN I WAS GROWING UP the tomato soup I had was Campbell's, and how I love it to this day. We used to have it on Sunday evenings with open-faced Cheddar cheese sandwiches. This is how my mother and I remember it, anyway. Bizarrely, my father and brother always fought us on the validity of this story, as if one would hide serving canned soup for dinner . . . anyway, I boringly digress . . . I have given the tomato soup of my youth an Italian makeover using the Slow-Roasted Tomatoes I always keep in the fridge. The condensed sweetness of the tomatoes really enriches the flavour and makes it incredibly kid friendly. Version two is the homage to Campbell, whoever he was . . .

3 tablespoons extra virgin olive oil

2 large cloves garlic, peeled and thinly sliced

4 fresh large basil leaves

2 400g cans whole peeled tomatoes with their juice

16 pieces (8 whole) Slow-Roasted Tomatoes (page 32), roughly chopped

Coarse salt

Freshly ground black pepper

Heat the olive oil in a large heavy saucepan over medium heat. Add the garlic and cook, stirring, for 2 minutes. Add the basil leaves, tomatoes and their juice and 1 can's worth of water (swish it around both cans to get out all of the tomato goodness). Bring to the boil, turn the heat to low and simmer uncovered for 40 minutes. Stir in the Slow-Roasted Tomatoes and season to taste with salt and pepper (about ½ teaspoon salt and ¼ teaspoon of pepper should do).

version one
4 tablespoons fresh basil leaves
Your best, highest-quality olive oil, for serving

For the first version, simply tear in the basil leaves and serve, drizzling each portion with your very best olive oil and a few extra grinds of black pepper.

version two
350ml milk
Your best, highest-quality olive oil, for serving
4 tablespoons fresh basil leaves, thinly sliced (chiffonade)

For the second version, stir in the milk and whizz the soup in a blender until it's completely smooth.
    Serve each portion with a drizzle of your very best olive oil and a bit of sliced basil.

SERVES: 4 • ACTIVE PREPARATION TIME: 20 minutes • TOTAL PREPARATION TIME: 1 hour

Version one

white bean soup: two ways

WHEN I WAS GROWING UP my father made his living writing, directing and producing television shows like *The White Shadow* and *St Elsewhere*. In Studio City, California, very near to the CBS studio where the shows were made, there was a fancy French restaurant called Le Serre where he used to take me when I would visit him at work (and on special occasions). I would always order French onion soup, really for just picking the crispy cheese from the sides of the pot. I've always loved the idea of French onion soup – the slow-cooked onions, the melted cheese – without actually liking it. I sought to make a vegetarian version with depth and flavour and more of an Italian slant. This simple one-pot soup makes a filling meal, and, just as I did, my kids love the melted, crispy cheese.

3 tablespoons extra virgin olive oil

1 fennel bulb, stems and fronds removed for another use, bulb thinly sliced

1 large onion, peeled and thinly sliced

2 large cloves garlic, peeled and thinly sliced

Pinch crushed chillies

¼ teaspoon dried oregano

¼ teaspoon freshly ground black pepper

2 410g cans cannellini beans, rinsed and drained

1l Vegetable Stock (page 36)

Coarse salt

Heat the olive oil in a large heavy soup pot over medium heat. Add the fennel and cook for 10 minutes, stirring occasionally. Add the onion and garlic, turn the heat as low as it can go, and cook for half an hour, stirring here and there. A little colour is OK, but you really want the vegetables to get soft and sweet. Add the crushed chillies, oregano and pepper and cook for a minute. Add the beans and stock, bring to the boil, lower to a simmer, add salt to taste and let cook on low heat for 1 hour. Proceed with either version.

version one (with kale)

1 bunch kale, stems discarded and leaves torn into bite-sized pieces
Your best, highest-quality olive oil, for serving

Stir in the kale leaves and let cook for 7 minutes, or until just cooked. Ladle into four bowls, drizzle with your very best oil and serve.

version two (french onion soup style)

8 thin slices baguette, toasted
75g Parmesan cheese, grated

Preheat the grill.

Ladle the soup into four ovenproof bowls. Float two toasts on each bowl and evenly distribute the cheese (yes it's a lot, but this is the time to be generous). Put the bowls under the grill until the cheese is bubbly, less than a minute.

SERVES: 4 • ACTIVE PREPARATION TIME: ½ hour • TOTAL PREPARATION TIME: 2 hours

Version one

fish stew

THIS STEW IS BASED ON a recipe in one of my favourite cookbooks, the *River Cafe Cookbook Easy*. I learned a lot about Italian flavours – especially the use of fennel seed as a secret ingredient – by cooking from the books by my friend Ruthie Rogers and her partner, the late, great Rose Gray. I make this easy, hearty fish stew often when friends come over. I'm not a fan of mussels (long story, Biarritz 2006) – but if you are, cut the clams down to a dozen and add a dozen mussels. Serve with bruschetta to sop up the juices.

3	tablespoons olive oil
4	cloves garlic, peeled and thinly sliced
	Pinch crushed chillies
	Pinch (about ¼ teaspoon) fennel seeds, crushed
8	small new potatoes, peeled, quartered and steamed for 7 minutes
2	400g cans whole peeled tomatoes with juice
	Coarse salt
	Freshly ground black pepper
250ml	dry white wine
450g	small clams, well scrubbed
6	heads-on langoustines, tiger prawns or other large prawns
225g	halibut or another firm, white fish, cut into 5 or 6 pieces
2	fillets red mullet or another strongly flavoured, oily fish (each 125–175g)
1	teaspoon grated peeled ginger
¼	juicy lemon
2	tablespoons chopped fresh parsley
	Your best, highest-quality olive oil, for serving

Heat the olive oil in a large heavy pan over medium-high heat with the garlic and cook, stirring, for 2 minutes, being careful not to burn the garlic. Add the crushed chillies and fennel and cook for another minute. Add the potatoes, tomatoes, a tomato can's worth of water and a large pinch of salt. Bring the mixture to the boil, turn the heat to low, cover it almost completely with a lid (let some steam escape from one side), and simmer for half an hour. Season the mixture to taste with salt and pepper. Add the white wine, turn the heat to high and boil for 3 minutes. Add the clams, langoustines and fish and sprinkle the grated ginger into the pan. Cover and cook over high heat for 5 minutes, or until the clams are opened and fish is just cooked through.

To serve, ladle into four bowls. Squeeze the lemon over each portion, sprinkle with parsley and drizzle a bit of your best olive oil on top. Serve with Bruschetta (page 212).

SERVES: 4 • ACTIVE PREPARATION TIME: ½ hour
TOTAL PREPARATION TIME: a little over 1 hour

gazpacho

I HAD MY FIRST BOWL of gazpacho when I was fifteen in Spain, and the impression it made was a lasting one. My Spanish 'Mama Julia' makes a great gazpacho (and everything else for that matter – she'll come up again in this book) and this version recalls hers. At the time I lived in Spain, families went out to work and school in the morning and converged back at the house for lunch, which Julia would make from scratch every day. Even then I remember marvelling at her ability to have a busy full-time job and yet come home and prepare a feast for seven during her lunch hour, sit down to eat, and go back out to the office for the rest of the afternoon, returning in the evening to do it again for dinner. For her it was just what was done and she did it with great ease and love. This soup is so fast and easy, no wonder it was a Mama Julia mainstay.

8	ripe vine-ripened tomatoes, peeled and cored
½	cucumber, peeled, seeded, and roughly chopped, plus more diced for serving
1	red Roasted Pepper (page 31)
½	red onion, peeled and diced, plus more diced for serving
2	cloves garlic, peeled and finely chopped
2	teaspoons coarse salt
½	teaspoon freshly ground black pepper
50g	1cm bread cubes, cut from day-old sourdough, rustic bread, ciabatta or the like
2	teaspoons red wine vinegar
2	tablespoons extra virgin olive oil
1	lime, halved
	Croutons, for serving

Combine the tomatoes, cucumber, roasted pepper, red onion, garlic, salt, pepper, bread, vinegar and olive oil in the blender and whizz away until it's as smooth as you like it. Chill for at least 1 hour before serving. Season to taste with more salt and the juice of the lime – you want enough acid to make it taste bright and fresh, but not limey. Serve with croutons, diced onion and cucumber.

tip on peeling the tomatoes Score the bottoms with a sharp paring knife and plunge them in boiling water for 30 seconds. Immediately put the tomatoes into an ice bath. The skins will slip right off. This method is also great for stone fruits like peaches and plums.

SERVES: 4 • **ACTIVE PREPARATION TIME:** 20 minutes
TOTAL PREPARATION TIME: 20 minutes plus at least 1 hour cooling

my spanish family

Ever since I was a kid I have had a fascination for Spain — I'm not quite sure where it came from. I remember hearing Spanish spoken all around me in both California and New York and always wanting to be a member of that warmhearted, life-loving Latino culture. One day in tenth-grade Spanish class, I heard about an opportunity to live in Spain as an exchange student and I jumped at the chance. From the spring day that I landed in Madrid, Spain — the land, the culture, the food, and mostly the people — has woven itself deeply into my heart and soul. The family that I lived with, the Lazaro family, became my second and very real family — and they are to this day. Julia, the matriarch, taught me so much about the importance of cooking for your loved ones. She continues to encourage and teach me, e-mailing me tips and recipes, much the way my father used to.

corn chowder

I LIKE TO MAKE THIS SOUP during our summers on Long Island, where the corn is abundant and sweet as can be. I love corn so much I tried to grow it one summer in the garden. The raccoons loved it even more. Now I stick to the gorgeous yield of the local farmers.

20g	unsalted butter
2	slices turkey bacon, finely diced
2	medium shallots, peeled and finely diced
½	large onion, peeled and finely diced
2	sprigs fresh thyme
1	bay leaf
	Kernels from 6 fresh corn cobs, cobs reserved
½	teaspoon coarse salt
¼	teaspoon freshly ground black pepper
500ml	Vegetable Stock (page 36)
250ml	milk
1	tablespoon finely chopped fresh chives, for garnish
1	teaspoon finely chopped fresh tarragon, for garnish

Melt the butter in a heavy soup pot over a medium heat. Add the bacon and cook, stirring, for 4 minutes, or until beginning to brown. Add the shallots, onion, thyme and bay leaf and cook for 5 minutes, stirring occasionally. Add the corn kernels, salt and pepper and cook for a minute, stirring everything together. Add the stock, milk and corn cobs, heat up and bring the soup to the boil. Lower the heat and simmer until the corn is cooked through, about 30 minutes. Remove the cobs, purée a ladleful of soup in the blender and return it to the pot. Season to taste with salt and pepper and serve, sprinkling each portion with a bit of the chives and tarragon.

note: You could make this with two rashers of pork bacon instead of the turkey bacon, in which case you won't need the butter.

make it vegan Substitute olive oil for the butter. Use a half teaspoon of pimenton instead of bacon. Sauté until fragrant. Continue with rest of recipe, and use soya-milk instead of regular milk.

 SERVES: 4 • ACTIVE PREPARATION TIME: ½ hour • TOTAL PREPARATION TIME: 40 minutes

salads

I was born and spent most of my childhood
in Southern California, where the produce was (and still is) from heaven.
My mother started taking me to the Santa Monica Farmers' Market (and
nearby recycling centre) in the 1970s. During the early 1980s I remember
greens becoming prominent on our plates and in our kitchen (we actually
had a patch of fresh wheatgrass growing and a press right there in the
kitchen – thank God my father kept 'Mallomars', chocolate marshmallows,
in the store cupboard to even things out). This early exposure to fresh greens
and veggies ensured my lifelong love for all things grown out of the ground
– and what better way to experience them but in salads, where they remain
intact and in the freshest state? For this reason I plant and try to maintain a
vegetable patch and take my kids to farmers' markets. When they get to pick
the vegetables themselves, they get a lot more excited about eating them.

miso dressing

I LOVE THIS MISO DRESSING. It works on salads, with veggies – even on grilled fish. Incredibly easy, it stores in the fridge for at least a week. I wish I were joking, but if there is a bowl of this dressing around and I am not looking, my son will stick his entire fist in and lick the dressing off as if it were cake batter. At least it's healthy . . .

½	mild onion, peeled and roughly diced
1	small or ½ large clove garlic, peeled and roughly chopped
75ml	white miso
2	tablespoons toasted sesame oil
35ml	soy sauce
2	tablespoons rice wine vinegar
2	tablespoons mirin
2	tablespoons water
	Large pinch coarse salt
	A few grinds black pepper
75ml	vegetable oil

Blitz everything but the vegetable oil together in a blender until smooth. While the blender is running, slowly stream in the oil. Season to taste with additional salt and pepper if needed.

 YIELD: 300ml · ACTIVE & TOTAL PREPARATION TIME: 5 minutes

balsamic & lime vinaigrette

THIS TANGY, SWEET DRESSING adds real zing to any grilled salad.
I have never served this without having a friend ask for the recipe!

2 tablespoons balsamic vinegar

2 tablespoons light agave nectar or honey

1 tablespoon fresh lime juice

100ml olive oil

Coarse salt

Freshly ground black pepper

Whisk the vinegar, agave and lime juice together in a bowl. Slowly whisk in the olive oil and season to taste with salt and pepper.

YIELD: 125ml

ACTIVE & TOTAL PREPARATION TIME: less than 5 minutes

standby vinaigrette

THIS BASIC DRESSING WILL NEVER let you down. My dad first gave me
the idea of maple syrup in salad dressings – it is a heavenly secret ingredient.

2 teaspoons Dijon mustard

2 teaspoons real Vermont maple syrup

60ml red wine vinegar

2 tablespoons vegetable or rapeseed oil

125ml extra virgin olive oil

Coarse salt

Freshly ground black pepper

Whisk together the mustard, maple syrup and vinegar. Slowly whisk in the oils and season to taste with salt and pepper.

YIELD: 200ml

ACTIVE & TOTAL PREPARATION TIME: less than 5 minutes

coarse mustard dressing

GRANARY MUSTARD IS A SPECIAL kind of mustard that is coarse and
seedy. I like getting the lovely authentic French brand in the ceramic jar and
using it for a variety of things – fresh bread with roast turkey and cornichons–
or this dressing. The texture of the mustard seeds really adds something
to a plate of chicory. This is inspired by the mustard dressing at the great
restaurant J. Sheekey in London. I used to order their salad of crisp, buttery
chicory with mustard dressing every night when coming offstage at London's
Donmar Warehouse in 2002.

3 tablespoons granary
mustard

4 teaspoons white wine
vinegar

Pinch granulated sugar
(shh!)

A few grinds black pepper

3 tablespoons extra virgin
olive oil

2 tablespoons vegetable oil

Whisk the mustard, vinegar, sugar and pepper together in a small bowl.
Slowly whisk in the oils.

YIELD: 125ml
ACTIVE & TOTAL PREPARATION TIME: less than 5 minutes

chive vinaigrette

THIS VERSATILE DRESSING LIVENS UP any salad. I use it on my niçoise
salad and on beautiful, fresh round lettuce to accompany roast chicken or fish.

1 teaspoon Dijon
mustard

1 teaspoon real Vermont
maple syrup

2 tablespoons white wine
vinegar

100ml extra virgin olive oil

2 tablespoons finely
chopped fresh chives

Coarse salt

Freshly ground black
pepper

Whisk together the mustard, maple syrup and vinegar. Slowly whisk in the
olive oil, fold in the chives and season to taste with salt and pepper.

YIELD: 125ml
ACTIVE & TOTAL PREPARATION TIME: 5 minutes

OPPOSITE, FROM TOP TO BOTTOM: Blue Cheese, Miso,
Coarse Mustard and Chive Vinaigrette dressings

blue cheese dressing

WHEN I WAS A SINGLE GAL in NYC and my parents lived in Westchester, we used to meet almost halfway for dinner at Gus's in Harrison, New York. It is a great bar serving delicious seafood and their salad was my favourite – red wine vinaigrette with big hunks of blue cheese. We were always a blue cheese-loving family and my version, with a creamy base (can't compete with Gus!), is fantastic on a wedge of iceberg lettuce or as a dip. It lasts for a good week in the fridge as well.

75ml	sour cream
75ml	Vegenaise/mayonnaise
50g	Gorgonzola cheese (use the *picante* or mountain kind, not the *dulce*), crumbled
75ml	cold water
4	teaspoons red wine vinegar
1	large shallot, peeled and thinly sliced
	Big pinch coarse salt
	A few grinds black pepper

Stir everything together in a small bowl.

YIELD: 350ml
ACTIVE & TOTAL PREPARATION TIME: 5 minutes

anchovy vinaigrette

A TWO-MINUTE DRESSING (if that) that adds tremendous flavour to bitter leaves. I adore this with escarole, I could eat it as a whole meal. This is my mother's favourite dressing, so I make it all the time for her by special request. I got my deep love of anchovies from her.

6	olive oil-packed Spanish anchovies
2	teaspoons Dijon mustard
2	tablespoons red wine vinegar
750ml	extra virgin olive oil
	Freshly ground black pepper

Whizz the anchovies, mustard, and vinegar together in a blender, being sure to get the anchovies completely puréed. With the motor on, slowly stream in the olive oil. Season to taste with pepper.

 YIELD: 125ml
ACTIVE & TOTAL PREPARATION TIME: less than 5 minutes

bitter leaf salad

FEW THINGS ARE AS HEALTHY for your liver as bitter greens – they
support its detoxification – and I love their taste. Living through the less than
fertile winter is mitigated by these gorgeous greens that grow through the cold
in some climate zones, allowing you to have a seasonal salad, even in winter.
I like to bundle my kids up and pick ours from our little veggie patch.

1 large head escarole or puntarelle or 2 heads radicchio, washed really well and torn into small pieces	Put the escarole in a large salad bowl and dress with the vinaigrette.
125ml Anchovy Vinaigrette (page 73)	

 SERVES: 4 · **ACTIVE & TOTAL PREPARATION TIME:** 10 minutes

'When we get older, we'll eat dinner together, right?'
—APPLE TO MOSES

chicory salad

THE SWEET, COARSE MUSTARD DRESSING is a nice complement to the bitter chicory, one of winter's real gifts.

4 small heads chicory, leaves separated

Coarse Mustard Dressing (page 71)

Stack the chicory leaves 'log cabin style' (i.e. to form a square) and evenly drizzle the mustard dressing over them.

 SERVES: 4 • **ACTIVE & TOTAL PREPARATION TIME:** 5 minutes

mizuna, tomato & avocado salad

THIS CRISP SALAD HAS AN ASIAN bent — miso and mizuna, a peppery Japanese leaf, combine beautifully.

4 large handfuls mizuna (totally OK to substitute round lettuce that's been roughly torn), washed

225g cherry tomatoes, washed and halved

1 avocado, peeled, stoned and diced

125ml Miso Dressing (page 68)

1 tablespoon sesame seeds

Put the mizuna on a large serving dish. Scatter the tomatoes and avocado over the mizuna. Drizzle with miso dressing and sprinkle with sesame seeds.

 **SERVES: 4** • **ACTIVE & TOTAL PREPARATION TIME:** 10 minutes

grilled radicchio
with gorgonzola

I MAKE THIS SALAD all the time in the summer when my barbecue is going.
With just a brush of olive oil and a nice strong cheese, you have a rich smoky
side dish in minutes.

2	heads radicchio, each cut into 6 wedges through the core
2	tablespoons extra virgin olive oil
¼	teaspoon freshly ground black pepper
225g	Gorgonzola *picante* cheese
	Your best, highest-quality olive oil, for serving
½	lemon, for serving

Preheat the barbecue over medium/low heat or turn on the grill if you're working inside.

In a large bowl, gently toss the radicchio with the olive oil to keep each wedge intact. Grill for 5 minutes, turning occasionally, or until starting to brown and soften (keep the heat moderate – you're not looking to char anything). If you're working with an indoor grill, remove the radicchio to a baking sheet, sprinkle with pepper, crumble over the cheese, and stick the sheet under the grill. If you're working outside, place the baking sheet on the grill or barbecue and simply close the lid. Watch closely so the cheese doesn't burn, you just want it to melt and bubble.

Serve, adding a healthy drizzle of your best olive oil and squeezing a bit of lemon juice over the radicchio.

 SERVES: 4 • ACTIVE & TOTAL PREPARATION TIME: 10 minutes

the wedge

A DRESSED WEDGE OF ICEBERG lettuce says American summer – I prefer
it with blue cheese, but vinaigrette works well if you are not into dairy. I like
mine plain, but feel free to dress yours up with sliced super ripe tomatoes or
thinly sliced onions. If there is a wedge with blue cheese dressing on a menu
anywhere, a Paltrow will be ordering it.

1	head iceberg lettuce, cut into 4 wedges
250ml	Blue Cheese Dressing (page 72)

Dress each wedge with plenty of dressing.

 SERVES: 4 • ACTIVE & TOTAL PREPARATION TIME: 5 minutes

marinated gigante bean salad with grilled prawns & watercress

THIS FILLING SALAD MAKES a great lunch. The giant beans are a delight – and kids think they are out of a fairy tale, they are so massive. The marinating time is key, so make sure you leave ample time to let it sit.

700g jar *la granja* beans (huge white butter beans from Navarra, Spain) or two 410g cans butter beans, rinsed and drained

1 large clove garlic, peeled and very thinly sliced

3 spring onions, thinly sliced

Freshly ground black pepper

Coarse salt

2 tablespoons of your best, highest-quality olive oil

16 large prawns (about 450g), peeled and de-veined

2 tablespoons extra virgin olive oil

2 bunches watercress, cleaned

1 lemon, halved

Combine the beans, garlic and spring onions in a large bowl. Sprinkle with a few grinds of pepper and a large pinch of salt. Drizzle your best olive oil over everything and stir to combine, being careful not to crush the beans. Let the beans rest in the refrigerator, covered, for at least an hour (preferably a few).

When you're ready to eat, coat the prawns with the extra virgin olive oil and season with a bit of salt and pepper. Barbecue over high heat for about 1½ minutes a side, or until firm to the touch and just coloured.

To serve, distribute the watercress, beans and warm prawns on four plates, squeezing a generous amount of lemon over each.

note: If you don't have access to a barbecue, heat a cast-iron pan under the grill and then grill the prawns in the smoking hot pan – this will mimic the charred crust you get by barbecuing and give you the crispy, caramelized edges that perfectly balance the soft beans.

SERVES: 4 as a first course • ACTIVE PREPARATION TIME: 15 minutes
TOTAL PREPARATION TIME: 15 minutes plus at least 1 hour marinating

classic chopped salad

BEING A NATIVE OF SOUTHERN CALIFORNIA, I have a deep love of
chopped salads, a dish that is served there often and in many variations.
This is a great main-course salad – the bacon and Gorgonzola are super rich
and delicious.

6   strips duck bacon (or
    whatever kind of bacon
    you love)

3   heads baby
    gem lettuce,
    2 hearts romaine or
    2 heads round lettuce,
    roughly chopped

1   ripe avocado, peeled,
    stoned, and diced

1   ripe large tomato,
    seeded and diced

50g Gorgonzola cheese,
     crumbled

125ml Standby Vinaigrette
       (page 69)

Cook the bacon in a frying pan until crispy. Drain on kitchen paper, cut off
and discard the fat if desired, and dice the crispy meat. Lay the lettuce down
on a big dish. Scatter the bacon, avocado, tomato, and Gorgonzola over the
lettuce in a mix or in rows, whatever you feel like. Dress with the vinaigrette.

  SERVES: 4 • ACTIVE & TOTAL PREPARATION TIME: 20 minutes

italian chopped salad

THIS WAS ONE OF THE FIRST salads I made, and I used to serve it up lots.
It's fantastic because you can adjust it to include whatever you have in the
fridge, or however it suits your fancy.

1	head leafy green lettuce, washed, dried and torn into small pieces
2	spring onions, thinly sliced on the bias
125g	cherry tomatoes, halved
3	preserved artichoke hearts from your favourite Italian delicatessen, cut into 1cm dice
4	bocconcini (small balls of mozzarella), cut into 1cm dice
	Large handful of haricots verts (thin green beans), ends trimmed, steamed for 7 minutes, and cut into 2.5cm pieces
1	red Roasted Bell Pepper (page 31), seeded and cut into 1cm dice
1	tablespoon Dijon mustard
2	teaspoons light agave nectar
5	olive oil-packed anchovies, finely diced
3	tablespoons red wine vinegar
125ml	extra virgin olive oil
	Coarse salt
	Freshly ground black pepper

Lay the lettuce down on a dish. Scatter the spring onions, tomatoes,
artichokes, bocconcini, haricots verts and roasted pepper over the lettuce.

For the dressing, whisk together the mustard, agave, anchovies and
vinegar. Slowly whisk in the olive oil and season to taste with salt and pepper.
Drizzle the dressing over the salad and serve.

 SERVES: 4 • ACTIVE & TOTAL PREPARATION TIME: ½ hour

cold niçoise salad

A TRUE CLASSIC. JUST PERFECT. If I am having friends over, often I won't assemble the salad in one bowl. I'll keep each item separate so people can make whatever version of the niçoise suits their eating proclivities. This is a real standby in the summer when we have people over for lunch.

4	175g tuna steaks
2	tablespoons extra virgin olive oil
	Coarse salt
	Freshly ground black pepper
12	small purple or new potatoes
150g	haricots verts (thin green beans) or regular green beans, ends trimmed
2	heads any soft, green lettuce, roughly torn
1	yellow Roasted Bell Pepper (page 31), torn into strips
1	red Roasted Bell Pepper (page 31), torn into strips
225g	cherry tomatoes, halved (if the tomatoes aren't super, it's best to slow roast them with a spoonful of extra virgin olive oil in a 140°C (275°F) gas 1 oven for a few hours)
75g	niçoise olives
4	organic large eggs, hard-boiled and cut into wedges
12	olive oil–packed Spanish anchovies
	Chive Vinaigrette (page 71)

Preheat the barbecue or grill to medium-high heat.

Rub the tuna steaks with the olive oil, season generously with salt and pepper and grill until cooked to your liking (I like mine cooked all the way through). Let the tuna cool for at least 10 minutes before cutting into 1cm-thick slices. Meanwhile, steam the potatoes for 20 minutes (or until cooked through) and the haricots verts for 7 minutes and let them cool. Cut the potatoes in half.

Arrange the lettuce on a big dish. Lay the haricots verts, peppers, tomatoes and olives over the lettuce. Arrange the potatoes and eggs round the edge. Lay the slices of tuna on top and criss-cross the anchovies over the whole thing. Drizzle with the vinaigrette.

  SERVES: 4 · ACTIVE & TOTAL PREPARATION TIME: ½ hour

hot niçoise salad

ONE COLD WINTRY DAY IN LONDON, I was dreaming about salad niçoise
– one of my favourites. It didn't seem right to be eating something so crispy
and chilly in the dead of winter, so I devised this hot version. It's a one-pan
dish and an easy clean-up. Perfect for when you are having friends for Sunday
lunch or dinner but you don't have hours to prep.

225g	green beans, ends trimmed
225g	cherry tomatoes, halved
75g	niçoise olives (preferably pitted)
7	tablespoons extra virgin olive oil
1	large handful fresh basil leaves
1	yellow Roasted Bell Pepper (page 31), roughly torn into strips
1	red Roasted Bell Pepper (page 31), roughly torn into strips
12	olive oil-packed Spanish anchovies
4	175g tuna steaks
	Coarse salt
	Freshly ground black pepper
4	organic large eggs
1	lemon, halved

Preheat the oven to 200°C (400°F) gas 6.

Steam the green beans for 4 minutes. Immediately toss them together in a large roasting tin with the tomatoes, olives and 4 tablespoons of the olive oil, crushing the tomatoes slightly with your hands. Tear in the basil and push the mixture around the perimeter of the tin. Nestle the peppers and anchovies in and around the vegetables. Lay the tuna steaks in the middle of the tin and coat each with ½ tablespoon of olive oil and rub with a generous amount of salt and pepper. Crack each egg into a small ramekin and tuck the ramekins into the corners of the tin. Drizzle each egg evenly with the remaining tablespoon of olive oil and sprinkle with salt and pepper. Stick the whole thing in the oven for 12 minutes, or until the eggs are just set and the tuna is cooked through but still moist. Pull the tin out, squeeze lemon over everything and serve.

  SERVES: 4 · ACTIVE & TOTAL PREPARATION TIME: 25 minutes

 You can arrange the whole thing early in the day and then throw it in the oven right before dinner.

rocket salad with smoked mozzarella & slow-roasted tomato crostini

THIS IS KIND OF a side dish-esque salad. The crostini act as mini pizzas for the kids. I do theirs with regular mozzarella and mine with the smoked variety.

12 thin slices baguette

Extra virgin olive oil

12 thin slices smoked mozzarella

6 halves (3 whole) Slow-Roasted Tomatoes (page 32), each half cut in half, at room temperature

50g baby rocket

1 tablespoon highest-quality balsamic vinegar

Coarse salt

Freshly ground black pepper

Preheat the grill.

Lay the slices of baguette on a baking sheet and drizzle each with a bit of olive oil. Put a slice of cheese on top of each baguette slice and run under the grill until the cheese is melted and bubbly (less than a minute). Top each crostini with a piece of tomato. Toss the rocket with a tablespoon of olive oil, the vinegar and salt and pepper to taste. Put the rocket on a dish and surround with the crostini.

 SERVES: 4 · ACTIVE & TOTAL PREPARATION TIME: 10 minutes

lobster club salad

A CHEF FRIEND OF MINE, Maxime, once prepared a salad a bit like this one. I was inspired by him to try my own version. It's pretty decadent – make it for a special summer lunch.

8 slices duck or turkey bacon (or whatever kind of bacon you love)

3 heads baby gem lettuce, 2 hearts romaine or 2 heads round lettuce, roughly torn

1 avocado, peeled, stoned, and diced

1.15kg cooked lobster meat (1 medium lobster or 2 lobster tails should do), finely chopped

225g cherry tomatoes, halved

125ml Chive Vinaigrette (page 71)

Cook the bacon in a frying pan until crispy. Drain on kitchen paper, cut off and discard the fat if desired, and dice the crispy meat. Arrange the lettuce on a dish. Nicely arrange the avocado, bacon, lobster and tomatoes on top (you can do this in rows or an artful scatter kinda thing). Drizzle the vinaigrette over the salad.

note: See note on page 110 for instructions on how to prepare the lobster.

 SERVES: 4 · ACTIVE & TOTAL PREPARATION TIME: 20 minutes

panzanella with roasted peppers, tomatoes & basil

WHENEVER I'VE LET GREAT BAKERY bread go stale by accident, I make this salad. The brightness of the tomato, roasted pepper and basil are really complemented by the texture of the bread.

175g stale rustic bread, cut into 2.5cm cubes

1 yellow Roasted Bell Pepper (page 31), roughly diced

1 red Roasted Bell Pepper (page 31), roughly diced

350g cherry tomatoes, quartered

2 tablespoons red wine vinegar

75ml extra virgin olive oil, plus more for serving

Coarse salt

Freshly ground black pepper

4 olive oil-packed Spanish anchovies, finely chopped

Large handful fresh basil leaves

Combine the bread, peppers and tomatoes together in a large bowl. Whisk the vinegar, olive oil, salt, pepper and anchovies together in a small bowl and drizzle over the salad. Tear in the basil, toss everything together with your hands and let sit for at least 15 minutes before serving. Distribute the panzanella on plates, drizzling each serving with a little extra olive oil.

SERVES: 4 • ACTIVE PREPARATION TIME: 15 minutes
TOTAL PREPARATION TIME: ½ hour

my ivy chopped salad

THIS SALAD IS INSPIRED BY the famous grilled vegetable salad at the Ivy restaurant in Los Angeles. This is one of my standbys – I make it for myself when the kids have gone to bed but it's equally good at a lunch party.

2	large beetroots
3	medium courgettes, sliced lengthways into 8mm-thick slices
2	fresh corn cobs, husks removed
1	bunch spring onions, dark green ends discarded
2	175g wild salmon fillets
	Extra virgin olive oil
	Coarse salt
2	heads round lettuce, leaves separated, washed and dried, and cut into thick strips
4	tablespoons fresh basil leaves, roughly torn
225g	cherry tomatoes, quartered
15g	fresh coriander leaves, roughly chopped
125ml	Balsamic & Lime Vinaigrette (page 69)
1	lime, quartered, for serving

Steam or boil the beetroots until cooked through, about 30 minutes. Let them sit until cool enough to handle and then peel them and cut into medium dice. Reserve.

Preheat the barbecue or grill to medium-low heat.

Rub the courgettes, corn, spring onions, and salmon with enough olive oil just to coat and sprinkle with salt. Grill the vegetables and fish until everything is nicely browned and cooked through, about 20 minutes. Cut the courgettes and spring onions into medium dice and reserve. Cut the corn off the cob and reserve. Break the salmon into large pieces with your hands and reserve.

Get a nice big dish and lay the lettuce down. Evenly and artfully scatter the basil, tomatoes, beetroots, corn, courgettes, spring onions, and coriander over the lettuce. Arrange the salmon along the edge of the dish. Drizzle the vinaigrette over the whole thing and serve the lime wedges alongside, encouraging your guests to use them.

SERVES: 4 · ACTIVE & TOTAL PREPARATION TIME: 40 minutes

You can prep all the ingredients ahead of time.

burgers
& sandwiches

My mother says that when she met my
father in 1969, he wouldn't eat a green vegetable and wouldn't stray
far from a hamburger or hot dog. Although this was a far cry from the
adventurous omnivore he became, the truth is, he never met a 'Hebrew
National' hot dog he didn't like and his love for cooking all started with
his grill. His grilling expertise began with the burger and over time gave
way to the mastery of delicate grilled fish, marinated chickens, lobsters and
experimentation with different wood chips.

He would buy the pre-marinated baby back ribs from the HoneyBaked
Ham store which came vacuum-packed and in rich barbecue sauce. The
whole family would go crazy for these things, which he cooked to the
perfect point of tenderness and caramelized crunch. I grew up standing next
to him bent over the barbecue at our house in Southern California, watching
his careful basting and his fury when something stuck to the surface, cursing
like a New York truck driver. The recipes in this chapter speak to the soul of
my 'dad as cook'. They are about satisfaction above all else.

tuna & ginger burgers

ONCE ON A FAMILY TRIP to Hawaii we stopped at a roadside restaurant right on the ocean. I fell in love with a creation I had never tried before, the tuna burger. The ones on Maui were done with Japanese-style pickled ginger on top. In this recipe, I put fresh ginger in with the tuna and let them sit overnight to really let the flavours fuse. I love a recipe where you can prepare it all ahead of time and then assemble it quickly just before you eat.

1	teaspoon wasabi powder
2	teaspoons Dijon mustard
1	teaspoon water
½	teaspoon freshly ground black pepper
½	teaspoon coarse salt
1	tablespoon peeled and finely chopped fresh ginger
1	tablespoon peeled and finely chopped garlic
1½	tablespoons groundnut oil, plus more for cooking
450g	highest-quality tuna, cut into 2.5cm pieces
2	tablespoons extra virgin olive oil
3	shallots, peeled and thinly sliced
4	wholemeal hamburger buns
125ml	Soy & Sesame Mayo (recipe follows)
	Handful fresh rocket

Combine the wasabi, mustard and water in a small bowl. Scrape it into a food processor along with the pepper, salt, ginger, garlic and groundnut oil. Pulse it all together to make a flavourful paste. Add the tuna and pulse just to combine – be careful not to overprocess the tuna as you want your burgers to have texture. Form the mixture into 4 burgers and set in the refrigerator for at least an hour (up to overnight) to let the flavours really settle in.

Meanwhile, heat the olive oil over medium-high heat in a frying pan. Add the shallots and sauté for about 10 minutes, until they get soft and sweet and a little brown. Reserve.

Preheat your barbecue or griddle pan over high heat.

Rub the tuna burgers with a little groundnut oil and grill for 2 or 3 minutes a side, to desired doneness. Grill the buns alongside the burgers. Spread the buns with the mayo, pile on the sautéed shallots and a bit of rocket and tuck in the burgers.

 SERVES: 4 · ACTIVE PREPARATION TIME: 15 minutes
TOTAL PREPARATION TIME: 15 minutes plus at least 1 hour chilling

The burgers can be formed and refrigerated.

soy & sesame mayo

THIS IS A GOOD TOPPING option for tuna burgers.

125ml	Vegenaise or mayo
2	teaspoons soy sauce
2	teaspoons toasted sesame oil

Whisk everything together.

 YIELD: 125ml · ACTIVE & TOTAL PREPARATION TIME: less than 5 minutes

cheesy stuffed burgers

I ORIGINALLY CAME UP WITH the 'stuffed' idea when filling a turkey burger with stuffing for a mini Thanksgiving recipe. I thought cheese would work well and, boy, does it. I like it with Gruyère, but kids definitely like something milder. You can use whatever cheese you've got in the fridge. Everyone in my house goes crazy for these things.

1	tablespoon extra virgin olive oil
1	onion, peeled and finely chopped
1	tablespoon very finely chopped fresh rosemary
450g	minced turkey or beef
½	teaspoon coarse salt
¼	teaspoon freshly ground black pepper
50g	cheese of your choice, coarsely grated
4	wholemeal hamburger buns

Heat the olive oil in a small frying pan over low heat. Add the onion and rosemary and cook for about 10 minutes, or until quite soft and sweet. Let the onion mixture cool a bit and then put it in a large mixing bowl with the turkey, salt and pepper. Mush the ingredients together with a wooden spoon or with your hands. Divide the mixture into quarters. Divide each quarter in half and form into 2 burgers. Place 2 tablespoons of cheese onto one burger and sandwich with the other, pinching the edges. Repeat this process with the remaining turkey and cheese.

Preheat your barbecue or grill to high.

Cook the burgers for 5 minutes on the first side, flip and cook for 4 more minutes, or until the burgers are browned and firm. Serve them on grilled wholemeal buns with all of your favourite fixings.

 SERVES: 4 · ACTIVE & TOTAL PREPARATION TIME: ½ hour

 The burgers can be formed and refrigerated.

home-made veggie burgers

AS MY DAUGHTER IS VEGETARIAN, I am always looking for creative ways to feed her. We once bought veggie burgers from a health food store that, upon cooking, became brown, rubbery and frankly terrifying. Sure that a home-made version could be created, I came up with this easy, super healthy version that Apple asks for weekly. My guys like these with avocado; I add ripe tomato and red onion and even pickled jalapeños to mine.

2	tablespoons extra virgin olive oil
1	small onion, peeled and finely diced
2	cloves garlic, peeled and finely chopped
¼	teaspoon ground cumin
½	teaspoon coarse salt
¼	teaspoon freshly ground black pepper
1	410g can black beans, drained and rinsed
75g	cooked brown rice
1	tablespoon finely chopped fresh coriander
2	tablespoons flour
3	tablespoons safflower oil
4	wholemeal hamburger buns

Heat the olive oil in a medium sauté pan over medium-low heat. Sauté the onion, garlic and cumin together until softened and fragrant, about 7 minutes. Add the salt, pepper, beans and rice and cook, stirring, for 2 minutes. Add the coriander and mash the mixture with a potato masher just to combine and get some cohesion – you want the burgers to have some texture.

Let the mixture cool until it's easy to handle. Form the mixture into 4 burgers. At this point, you can set the burgers in the fridge for a few hours. Dust on both sides with flour. Heat the safflower oil in a large frying pan over medium-high heat and brown the burgers on both sides, about a minute on each side. Serve them on grilled wholemeal buns with all of your favourite fixings.

SERVES: 4 • ACTIVE PREPARATION TIME: 25 minutes
TOTAL PREPARATION TIME: 25 minutes plus at least 10 minutes cooling

portobello & slow-roasted tomato burgers

HERE IS ANOTHER DELICIOUS VEGETARIAN burger option to serve.
Portobello mushrooms with their meaty flavour really come alive with the
Slow-Roasted Tomatoes and smoked mozzarella combo, but you can dress
them up any way you like. And believe it or not, even kids love them . . .
just feel free to leave out the 'mushroom' word.

125ml extra virgin olive oil

2 cloves garlic, peeled and crushed

Pinch coarse salt

A few grinds black pepper

Juice of 1 lemon

4 large portobello mushrooms

1 sweet onion, peeled and cut into thick slices

4 wholemeal hamburger buns

8 halves (4 whole) Slow-Roasted Tomatoes (page 32)

A few slices smoked mozzarella

Small handful fresh rocket or 4 soft lettuce leaves, for serving

Combine half the olive oil with the garlic, salt, pepper and lemon juice in a shallow bowl. Cut 3 slits through the top of each mushroom, being sure not to cut all the way through. Coat the mushrooms in the mixture and let them sit for about 15 minutes, being sure to get some of the mixture in the slits.

Heat the barbecue to low.

Grill the mushrooms, turning occasionally, for 15 minutes, or until softened and a bit browned.

Remove the mushrooms to a baking sheet and preheat the grill. Turn the barbecue up to medium high, coat the onion slices with 2 tablespoons of olive oil, and grill for about 2 minutes a side, or until slightly softened and browned. Cut the buns in half and grill alongside if you wish. Drizzle the cut side of the buns with the remaining olive oil and sprinkle with coarse salt.

Top each mushroom with the Slow-Roasted Tomatoes, grilled onion and smoked mozzarella. Run under the grill until just melted and serve in the buns with a bit of rocket.

make it vegan Omit the smoked mozzarella. See page 102 for another vegan version.

 SERVES: 4 · ACTIVE PREPARATION TIME: 25 minutes · TOTAL PREPARATION TIME: 40 minutes

asian portobello burgers

THIS BURGER OF PORTOBELLO MUSHROOM basted with soy sauce and sesame oil is a delicious vegan version. The trick with portobellos is cooking them for a long time over low heat, concentrating their meaty flavour.

2	tablespoons soy sauce
4	portobello mushrooms
125ml	toasted sesame oil
4	brioche or wholemeal hamburger buns, toasted
125ml	Soy & Sesame Mayo (page 96)
	Handful fresh mizuna or rocket

Drizzle the soy sauce on both sides of the mushrooms and then brush each side with sesame oil. Let them sit for at least 10 minutes – this is a good time to preheat the barbecue or grill to low.

Grill the mushrooms, turning occasionally, for 15 minutes, or until softened and a bit browned.

Brush the cut sides of the buns with sesame oil and spread with the mayo. Place the portobellos into the buns along with a few leaves.

 SERVES: 4 • ACTIVE PREPARATION TIME: 25 minutes • TOTAL PREPARATION TIME: 40 minutes

duck & rosemary burgers with plum ketchup

THIS IS INSPIRED BY the best duck burger I ever had at the Melrose Bar and Grill in Los Angeles. I have been known to drive there directly from the airport to have one with fries and a good glass of California pinot noir. The restaurant recently closed, but I rustled this version up in my own kitchen. It's almost as good as the original.

450g minced duck breast (if you have a nice butcher, he should be able to do this — it's about 2 regular-sized skinless duck breasts, minced), at room temperature

½ teaspoon coarse salt

¼ teaspoon freshly ground black pepper

1 tablespoon very finely chopped fresh rosemary

4 wholemeal hamburger buns

Plum Ketchup (recipe follows)

Preheat the barbecue or grill to medium high.

Thoroughly mix the duck with the salt, pepper and rosemary. Form the mixture into 4 burgers, each about 1.5cm thick. Grill for 5–6 minutes a side, or until firm to the touch — I like them quite well done, but cook them to your liking. Meanwhile, cut the buns in half and grill them alongside the burgers just until they're golden brown. While the burgers rest, slather the buns with Plum Ketchup, and sandwich in the burgers.

 SERVES: 4 · ACTIVE & TOTAL PREPARATION TIME: 15 minutes

 The burgers can be formed and refrigerated.

plum ketchup

THIS TAKES TWO SECONDS and really works on duck burgers. It works on turkey burgers too.

4 tablespoons ketchup

4 tablespoons plum jam

Stir the ketchup and jam together.

 YIELD: 125ml · ACTIVE & TOTAL PREPARATION TIME: less than 5 minutes

crab cake burgers with spicy remoulade

ONE DAY MY *SPONGEBOB SQUAREPANTS*-WATCHING son asked me what a krabby pattie was. I gathered that it was a sort of crab cake burger and so I endeavoured to make one. Man, are these things good. I slather them with my home-made Spicy Remoulade and please a crowd. It's even a hit with kids.

2	tablespoons extra virgin olive oil
3	large shallots, peeled and finely diced
450g	coarse crabmeat
2	tablespoons finely chopped fresh parsley
1	lemon, zested and then cut in half
2	medium eggs, beaten together
175ml	Vegenaise or mayo
	Big pinch coarse salt
	A few grinds black pepper
100g	fresh breadcrumbs
3	tablespoons safflower oil
4	brioche buns, toasted
	Spicy Remoulade (page 105)

Heat the olive oil in a small frying pan over medium heat. Add the shallots and cook, stirring, for about 5 minutes, or until just softened. Let the shallots cool. In a large bowl, using your hands or a wooden spoon, combine the shallots with the crab, parsley, lemon zest, eggs, Vegenaise, salt, pepper and breadcrumbs. Form the mixture into 4 burgers, wrap each one tightly with clingfilm, and set in the fridge for at least 2 hours, up to overnight. When you're ready to eat, heat the safflower oil over medium-high heat in a large frying pan. Cook the burgers until browned on both sides, about 1½ minutes per side.

Squeeze a bit of lemon over each burger and serve on the toasted buns spread generously with Spicy Remoulade.

 SERVES: 4 • ACTIVE PREPARATION TIME: 25 minutes
TOTAL PREPARATION TIME: 25 minutes plus at least 2 hours chilling

spicy remoulade

THIS TOPPING IS CREAMY, TANGY and spicy, bringing a zing to seafood.
It's also great as a dip for fish fingers.

250ml	Vegenaise or mayo
10	cornichons, finely chopped
2	tablespoons peeled and finely chopped onion
1	teaspoon Lee's Home-made Sriracha (page 35) or commercial sriracha, or to taste
¼	teaspoon freshly ground black pepper
	Juice of ½ lemon

Stir everything together.

 YIELD: 250ml • ACTIVE & TOTAL PREPARATION TIME: less than 5 minutes

'Kiddish' food.
—MOSES

grilled tuna rolls

I BASICALLY LOVE ANYTHING that comes in a hot dog bun . . . except hot dogs (sorry, Dad). I mean, what the heck is in those things? Anyway, inspired by the glorious East Coast tradition of fish deliciousness in a bun, I made these one summer when I had tuna steaks in the fridge for dinner but had an unexpected group of hungry lunch guests. The tuna stretches really far in the hot dog buns and the vinaigrette really makes it pop.

2 tablespoons sweet white miso paste

1 tablespoon vegetable, sunflower or rice bran oil

1 tablespoon light agave nectar

1 teaspoon water

1 tablespoon rice wine vinegar

Pinch fine salt

2 1cm-thick tuna steaks or 1 large tuna steak, cut in half horizontally

2 tablespoons sesame seeds

4 hot dog buns

1 head round lettuce, leaves separated

4 tablespoons Shallot & Coriander Vinaigrette (page 107), for serving

2 tablespoons fresh coriander leaves, for serving

Preheat the barbecue or a griddle pan over high heat.

Whisk together the miso, oil, agave, water and rice wine vinegar. Season to taste with salt. Rub the tuna steaks all over with the mixture and place on the grill or pan. Evenly sprinkle 1 tablespoon of the sesame seeds on the fish. Grill on the first side for 3 minutes, flip, and sprinkle the cooked sides with the remaining sesame seeds. Grill for an additional 3 minutes and then remove to a plate. I like the tuna to be just cooked through, but feel free to grill for less time if you prefer it medium or even rare.

To serve, grill or toast the buns. Lay a few lettuce leaves on the bottom half of each bun. Cut the tuna into 1cm slices across the grain and evenly distribute on the lettuce. Drizzle each sandwich with a tablespoon of the vinaigrette, being sure to get plenty of sliced shallots in each spoonful, and sprinkle with the coriander leaves. Close each sandwich with the top halves of the buns and serve with lots of napkins.

 SERVES: 4 · ACTIVE & TOTAL PREPARATION TIME: 20 minutes

shallot & coriander vinaigrette

2½ tablespoons rice wine
   vinegar

1 tablespoon light agave
   nectar

1 tablespoon soy sauce

4 tablespoons vegetable or
   sunflower oil

   A few dashes chilli sesame
   oil or your favourite hot
   sauce

2 shallots, peeled and very
   thinly sliced

1 tablespoon roughly
   chopped fresh coriander

Whisk the vinegar, agave and soy sauce together. While whisking, drizzle in the vegetable oil. Add the hot pepper sesame oil to taste and stir in the shallots and coriander. If you make this in advance, be sure to stir it well before serving.

YIELD: 175ml • ACTIVE & TOTAL
PREPARATION TIME: less than 5 minutes

grilled tuna & gruyère sandwiches

WHEN I WAS A TEENAGER growing up in New York City, I spent most of my allowance at two places: an establishment called Jackson Hole (and the other I don't think I can disclose). These are family-owned greasy spoons where we would gather to be taught how to swear in Greek by the borderline-handsome guys who worked there, smoke cigarettes and, if it was early in the week, eat tuna melts on rye bread. Since my high school days I have been a devotee of the NYC-style tuna melt. For my home version I do them with Gruyère and a country-style bread from the bakery, but anything works. For the kids I use a milder cheese like Emmental or Cheddar. I like to serve with great potato crisps and sweet-and-sour pickles.

350g	best-quality canned or jarred tuna packed in olive oil
100ml	Vegenaise or mayo
1	teaspoon Dijon mustard
	Large pinch celery seeds
	Freshly ground black pepper to taste
8	slices freshly baked country bread
50g	Gruyère cheese, grated
25g	unsalted butter

Mix the tuna, 4 tablespoons Vegenaise, mustard, celery seeds and pepper together in a small bowl. Spread the remaining Vegenaise on 4 slices of the bread. Divide the tuna between these 4 slices and evenly scatter the cheese on top of the tuna. Sandwich with the remaining 4 slices of bread. Melt the butter in your largest non-stick frying pan (or in 2 medium frying pans) over medium-high heat. Fry the sandwiches for a minute on the first side, or until the bread is golden. Turn the sandwiches, put a lid on the pan, and cook for an additional minute. Cut each sandwich in half and serve.

 SERVES: 4 • ACTIVE & TOTAL PREPARATION TIME: 10 minutes

 You can make the tuna salad ahead of time.

turkey BLTs

I GREW UP SPENDING THE SUMMERS in Williamstown, Massachusetts, going to tennis camp while my mother was rehearsing plays at Williamstown Theatre. Every day my father would take my brother and me to the Williams College 'commons', now known as the 'snack bar'. Every day I ate a BLT on that crazily spongy supermarket bread, French fries and a milkshake. Wow. I haven't lost my love for these incredibly American sandwiches and I make them constantly. I'm not sure how healthy bacon is in general, but I know it's incredibly delicious.

8	slices organic turkey bacon (or whatever kind of bacon you love)
8	slices wholemeal sandwich bread
125ml	Vegenaise or mayo
	Coarse salt
	Freshly ground black pepper
	Handful baby rocket or 4 leaves round or romaine lettuce
2	tablespoons extra virgin olive oil
8	halves (4 whole) Slow-Roasted Tomatoes (page 32) or 8 slices fresh ripe tomato

Cook the bacon in a large frying pan over medium-high heat until crispy on both sides. Drain on kitchen paper and cut each slice in half. Meanwhile, toast the bread.

Spread one side of each slice of bread with 1 tablespoon of Vegenaise. Sprinkle each slice with a tiny pinch of salt and a grind of black pepper. Evenly distribute the rocket on 4 slices of bread, drizzle each with ½ tablespoon of olive oil and sprinkle with a bit more salt and pepper. Lay 2 tomato halves on top of each heap of rocket, squishing them a bit so that they cover most of the surface. Overlap 4 pieces of turkey bacon on each sandwich (each sandwich is entitled to 2 whole slices). Top each sandwich with the spare piece of Vegenaise-slathered bread, cut in half and serve.

make it vegan   You can substitute fried tempeh bacon to make a delicious vegan version.

 SERVES: 4 • ACTIVE & TOTAL PREPARATION TIME: 15 minutes

lobster rolls

ONE OF MY BEST FRIENDS from my high school days married his beautiful bride in Maine, and we all made the trip up to that gorgeous part of the country. The night we arrived, some of us went to a remote waterside restaurant and ate the best lobster rolls of all time – local eating up there. We were tired from the trip and freezing cold even though it was July (does it ever warm up in Maine?) but those succulent sandwiches and reminiscent laughter left us happy. I have chased that lobster roll ever since. The secret here is the little bit of white miso, which complements the sweetness of the lobster meat.

125ml	Vegenaise or mayo
1	teaspoon Dijon mustard
2	teaspoons white miso mixed together with 2 teaspoons boiling water
	Pinch coarse salt
	A few grinds of black pepper
2	teaspoons finely chopped fresh tarragon (optional)
1.15kg	lobster meat, roughly chopped
4	top-split hot dog buns, toasted and brushed with 25g unsalted butter, melted
1	tablespoon finely chopped fresh chives

Whisk together the Vegenaise, mustard, miso mixture, salt, pepper and tarragon if using. Fold in the lobster meat. Divide the salad evenly into the buns (it's OK if they overflow a bit). Top each sandwich with a sprinkle of chives and serve.

note: One small lobster will yield about 500g meat. I cook my lobsters by boiling them for 9 minutes and then dousing them in cold water to stop the cooking. I use a mallet to crack the shells (much easier than a lobster cracker!).

If you like, make a quick lobster stock with the shells (cover them with water and simmer about 20–25 minutes with a few aromatics like a leek and bay leaf) and store it in the freezer – a luxurious substitute for Fish Stock (page 40) and especially good for a risotto.

  SERVES: 4 generously · ACTIVE & TOTAL PREPARATION TIME: 10 minutes

You can make the lobster salad ahead of time.

playwright's melt

LENNY GERSHE AUTHORED *BUTTERFLIES ARE FREE*, in which my mother first acted on Broadway (in 1969), and for which she won the Tony. He also authored the recipe for this gooey, lovely grilled cheese-type thing that my parents used to make all the time. My mother says that this was a mainstay in our house whenever people stopped by for lunch. Perfect with soup or a salad as well.

40g brine-cured black olives, roughly chopped

4 spring onions, finely sliced

75g Cheddar cheese, coarsely grated

1 teaspoon curry powder

A few dashes Worcestershire sauce

2 tablespoons Vegenaise or mayo

4 English muffins, split and toasted

Mix all the ingredients except the English muffins and spread the mixture evenly on the muffins. Run them under the grill until browned and bubbling, about a minute.

note: If you don't like the salty pungency of brine-cured black olives, you can make this a bit milder by using what Lenny Gershe traditionally used – a small can of semi-flavourless black olives. A little kitsch never hurt anyone.

 SERVES: 4 • **ACTIVE & TOTAL PREPARATION TIME:** 10 minutes

fried sole sandwiches with spicy mayo & pickles

THESE ARE HEAVEN — FRIED SOLE on a fresh baguette — how can you go wrong? I always make the sandwiches for us and fry the sole in little strips for the kids, the perfect fish finger.

3	fillets Dover sole, rinsed and patted dry with kitchen paper
250ml	milk
100g	dry breadcrumbs mixed with 1 teaspoon each coarse salt and freshly ground black pepper
4	tablespoons extra virgin olive oil
1	lemon
	Spicy Mayo (recipe follows)
1	baguette, cut in half lengthways (remove some of the middle if it's a very bready baguette)
25g	baby rocket or shredded romaine lettuce
8	tablespoons sliced dill pickle

Dip the fish in the milk and then dredge it in the breadcrumbs. Meanwhile, heat the olive oil in a large non-stick frying pan over medium-high heat. Cook the fish for 2 minutes on each side, in batches if necessary. Drain on kitchen paper; cut the lemon in half and squeeze the juice from one half over the fish.

While the fish is cooking, slather the mayo on the cut sides of the bread and lay the rocket and pickles evenly on one side. Cut the fish fillets in half lengthways and evenly layer them on top of the rocket and pickles. Sandwich with the other piece of baguette, cut into quarters and serve with the remaining half of the lemon cut into wedges.

 SERVES: 4 • ACTIVE & TOTAL PREPARATION TIME: 15 minutes

spicy mayo

THIS SPICY MAYO IS REALLY GOOD. I omit the sriracha for the kids.

250ml	Vegenaise or mayo
1½	tablespoons ketchup
1½	tablespoons Lee's Home-made Sriracha (page 35)

Mix everything together.

 YIELD: 300ml
ACTIVE & TOTAL PREPARATION TIME: less than 5 minutes

vietnamese prawn sandwiches

MARINATING THE PRAWNS not only packs in the flavour, but it also helps them caramelize as they cook on the grill. The smoky, sweet prawns combined with the tang and spice of the sauces and the crunchy baguette make for an incredible layering of different tastes and textures.

4   large prawns, or 1 large lobster tail, or 450g cleaned squid, peeled, de-veined, and cut in half lengthways (butterflied)

2   tablespoons soy sauce

2   tablespoons toasted sesame oil

1   teaspoon peeled and grated ginger

2   small carrots, peeled and coarsely grated

½   teaspoon coarse salt

½   teaspoon granulated sugar

4   tablespoons rice wine vinegar

125ml   Vegenaise or mayo

Lee's Home-made Sriracha (page 35), to taste

Juice of 1 lime

1   baguette, cut in half lengthways

½   cucumber, peeled, seeds removed, and cut into matchsticks

Handful fresh coriander leaves

Handful fresh basil leaves

Put the prawns in a small bowl with the soy sauce, sesame oil and ginger and stir to combine. Cover and let sit in the refrigerator for at least 1 hour. Combine the carrots, salt, sugar and vinegar in another small bowl, cover and let sit in the refrigerator for at least 1 hour. In a third small bowl, combine the Vegenaise, sriracha and lime juice, cover and let sit in the refrigerator for at least 1 hour.

Preheat the barbecue or a griddle pan over medium-high heat.

Grill the prawns for 2 minutes a side, remove from the heat and let rest while you grill the baguette halves on all sides until lightly toasted. Slather the cut sides of the baguette with the Vegenaise mixture. Layer the cucumber, pickled carrots, and herbs on one side of the baguette. Cut the prawns on the bias into 1cm-thick slices and lay them on top of the vegetables and herbs. Sandwich with the other piece of baguette, cut into quarters and serve.

note: If you don't have access to a barbecue, heat a cast-iron pan under the grill and then grill the prawns in the smoking hot pan – this will mimic the charred crust you get by barbecuing.

 SERVES: 4 • ACTIVE PREPARATION TIME: 20 minutes
TOTAL PREPARATION TIME: 1 hour and 20 minutes

You can prepare all the elements ahead of time.

oyster po'boys

MY FATHER WENT TO TULANE University in New Orleans, Louisiana, in the 60s and the stories from that time were legendary. He and his fraternity brothers got into all kinds of mischief including setting up a mini casino in the frat house. With the money they made they switched from beer to spirits. Known to the boys at Sammy (Sigma Alpha Mu) as the cure for all hangovers, the po'boy became their staple diet. When I went to NOLA for the first time when my brother was in attendance at Tulane, my father took me to his favourite po'boy joint with no tables. I'm not sure if it's still standing, but it opened my eyes to the glory of this special, very American sandwich.

500ml	groundnut or safflower oil, for frying
1	dozen oysters, shucked (you can get your fishmonger to do this or gently steam them for 5 minutes first to make it easier)
250ml	buttermilk
100g	dry breadcrumbs
	Coarse salt
¼	lemon
1	soft baguette, cut in half lengthways
125ml	Vegenaise or mayo
125ml	of your favourite cocktail sauce (preferably with lots of horseradish)
75g	romaine lettuce leaves, shredded
2	very ripe tomatoes, thinly sliced
1	pickled cucumber, thinly sliced (optional)

Heat the groundnut oil in a deep-fat fryer or large heavy saucepan to 190°C (375°F).

Dip the oysters into the buttermilk and then dredge them in the breadcrumbs. Fry for about 25 seconds on each side, or until super crispy and browned. Drain on kitchen paper and sprinkle each oyster with salt and a tiny bit of lemon juice.

Slather the cut side of one baguette half with Vegenaise and slather the other with cocktail sauce. Evenly distribute the lettuce, tomatoes and pickled cucumber on the bottom half and then top with the oysters. Sandwich with the top half of the baguette, cut into quarters and serve to lucky friends.

make it vegan   Replace the oysters with similar amounts of tofu or peeled, sliced aubergine. For the aubergine version, the aubergine should be sweated first: slice into 1cm-thick rounds, place them on kitchen-paper-lined baking sheets, and scatter Maldon salt on both sides of each slice. Then place more kitchen paper on top and leave the slices to sweat. After 30 minutes, remove the paper, then rinse and dry aubergine slices and cut into cubes. Heat 1cm of groundnut oil in a deep-fat fryer or large, heavy saucepan over high heat. Lightly dredge the aubergine slices in flour. Add floured aubergine slices in a single layer. Turn heat to medium and cook 1½ minutes on both sides. Drain on kitchen paper. Repeat in batches as needed.

SERVES: 4 • ACTIVE & TOTAL PREPARATION TIME: 20 minutes

fried clam rolls

I GREW UP GOING TO the island of Nantucket (off the coast of Massachusetts) at the end of every summer. My brother and I were allowed to roam around with other kids and have our first taste of freedom – taking walks and playing in the sun, with the smell of box hedge and salt air on our summer skin. We stayed in a cottage near the harbour and explored the island on mopeds. I usually rode on the back of my mother's moped, and my brother went with my dad. We would find empty beaches and spend the day in the surf, jumping in a nearby freshwater pond before going to our favourite lunch spot, Rhoda's Roadside – a fish shack on the side of the road. The clams were fresh from the island, battered and perfectly fried, topped with home-made tartar sauce, and with French fries on the side. My love for the clam roll was born at Rhoda's. I now make them at home.

500ml	groundnut or safflower oil, for frying
4	dozen clams, shucked, rubbery end discarded
250ml	evaporated milk
125g	unbleached plain flour
	Coarse salt
4	brioche rolls, toasted
125ml	Vegenaise or mayo
½	quantity Deli Coleslaw (page 201)

Heat the groundnut oil in a heavy saucepan with tall sides until a pinch of flour sizzles upon contact, about 190°C (375°F).

Meanwhile, cut each clam in half, submerge it in the evaporated milk and then dredge it with flour. Carefully slip the clams into the hot oil and cook for about 45 seconds on each side, or until dark golden brown. Be careful, as clams have a lot of moisture that can make the oil pop – the taller the edges on your pan, the safer you'll be. Drain the clams on a kitchen-paper-lined plate and sprinkle with a few pinches of coarse salt. Slather the buns with Vegenaise, evenly distribute the coleslaw in the rolls, and then pile them high with fried clams.

 SERVES: 4 • ACTIVE & TOTAL PREPARATION TIME: 20 minutes

pastas

When people talk about 'family style' food,
I always envision a scene out of a Scorsese movie, people delving into a large
platter of spaghetti and meatballs and feeling very jovial and happy and yelling
over each other. Pasta has become an American comfort food and for good
reason: home-made fresh, dried, from the deli freezer – it's got a major ease to
deliciousness ratio. When I look at plain pasta I see opportunity, I smell cheese,
I dream of the wine that will accompany it. It's easy, it's fast and it's kind of
unbeatable. It's perfect for families; you can always amend the preparation
for kids – they are happy with just butter and Parmesan. Many of these sauces
are done and ready in the time it takes to boil the water and cook the pasta –
just the thing when you come home from work or you've tucked the kids in
and you want a quick but really good dinner. While each of the recipes in
this section is delicious and dependable, the crown jewel is the Duck Ragu
(page 138), a recipe I worked on for years to recall a special night in Tuscany.
It brings me back there every time.

A few days after my thirtieth birthday, my father and I took a culinary road trip that started in Umbria and wound its way into Tuscany. We rented a car and began our unique trip, meeting up for lunch with his best friend from Tulane in Pienza, touring the Uffizi before it opened, stopping at any great restaurant, museum or church along the way. One night the two of us found ourselves in a little town called Cortona. My father wasn't feeling well, but we decided to go to a local village tavern for dinner. Arm in arm we walked up and down hills and over cobblestones in the early autumn air until we got to the old and beautiful restaurant, where we were warmly greeted and given delicious plates of hand-rolled pici with heavenly duck ragu. When I look back at that dinner now I realize that my father, who would die only three days later, set me up for the rest of my life with the wisdom he imparted that night. He talked to me about the importance of knowing who I was, of respecting myself, my drive, my heart. He spoke about his long love for my mother, the importance of the degree of freedom in their marriage – letting the other person breathe while being their biggest supporter. And he spoke of the joy that his children had brought him, saying his only regret in life was not having had more. As we walked back to the hotel that night, I never could have fathomed that it would be our last meal, just the two of us. I thought that he would always be there to guide me, to push me further. The clear love and devotion I felt from him that night has not left me and I suspect it never will.

fresh pasta

MAKING FRESH PASTA IS ONE of the simplest things to do at home –
provided you have the right equipment. I kept reading how easy it was to do
and then one day I just worked up the courage to try it. The first model of pasta
maker I tried was Jamie Oliver's hand-cranked pasta maker, which is great, but
then I discovered the electric KitchenAid pasta attachment and I never looked
back. My kids LOVE to participate in this project – they hold the pasta up as
it's fed through the machine. You can slice the pasta into strips of any width
(spaghetti, fettuccine, pappardelle, etc.) or tear the sheets into pieces for a
rustic, easy pasta. Also, it's great to make egg white omelettes, meringues, angel
food cake or Blueberry Pavlovas (page 258) with all the leftover egg whites.

2	organic large eggs
10	organic large egg yolks
300g	00 pasta flour or 225g unbleached plain flour, plus more for kneading and dusting

Whisk together the whole eggs and yolks in a bowl. Put the flour on a large
board or in your biggest mixing bowl, make a well in the centre and pour
the eggs into the well. Slowly bring in the flour using a fork and then knead
by hand just a few times or until a nice dough forms. Add a bit more flour if
the dough is very sticky (it's always a little different depending on the size of
your eggs, humidity, etc.). Let the dough rest under a tea towel for at least
10 minutes before proceeding.

Now take out your pasta machine. Cut the dough into 8 pieces and
roughly form into rectangles. Dust each rectangle with a bit of flour. Starting
on the widest setting, put one piece through the machine, dusting with more
flour if it's at all sticky. Fold the dough over itself and go through again on
the same setting (you are essentially kneading and stretching the dough).
Repeat this process on each setting, going from widest to thinnest, until you
are left with a long, thin sheet of pasta. Be gentle during the process and be
careful not to tear your sheets. Repeat the whole process with all the pieces
of dough, laying them on your clean worktop as you finish them and covering
them with clingfilm or a barely damp tea towel. Proceed with ravioli or cut
the pasta into shapes, tossing it with a bit of flour to keep it from sticking.

 SERVES: 4–6 · ACTIVE & TOTAL PREPARATION TIME: 2 hours

spaghetti alla vongole

SUCH A CLASSIC. IN MY VERSION, the little bit of anchovy, tomato and fennel seed are key since they add an incredible depth of flavour. You can also serve these clams on their own without the pasta – just be sure to have plenty of good, crusty bread either way to sop up all the delicious juice.

3	tablespoons extra virgin olive oil
2½	cloves garlic, peeled and thinly sliced
	Pinch crushed chillies (use to your liking, the ones I buy in London are particularly spicy, so a little goes a long way)
	Pinch fennel seeds
6	olive oil-packed Spanish anchovies
225g	cherry tomatoes
175ml	dry white wine, such as a sauvignon blanc
900g	fresh small clams or cockles, rinsed and scrubbed (See Salt Scrubs for Clams, page 43)
6	fresh large basil leaves, roughly chopped
350g	spaghetti

Heat the olive oil in a large sauté pan over low heat. Add the garlic, crushed chillies, and fennel seeds and cook for just a minute, or until warmed and beginning to soften. Add the anchovies and stir them until they melt into the oil, about a minute. Crush the tomatoes gently by hand, just so that their skins burst and add them to the pan. Cook for about 3 minutes, crushing with the back of your spoon, until the tomatoes begin to break down. Add the wine, turn the heat up and boil for a minute. Add the clams, cover the pan and cook until the clams open, about a minute or two. Uncover the pan and lower the heat to simmer to let the sauce reduce until it's thick enough to just coat a spoon (you want it to really stick to the pasta). Turn off the heat and add the basil.

Meanwhile, cook your spaghetti until perfectly al dente. Add it to the pan with the sauce and stir to coat it.

To serve, divide the pasta between four pasta bowls, spooning the clams and all their yummy bits on top of each portion.

 SERVES: 4 • ACTIVE & TOTAL PREPARATION TIME: 20 minutes

penne puttanesca

THIS IS REALLY, REALLY GOOD. If young kids are involved, just serve theirs with the tomato sauce. I throw in some olives for my daughter – she loves olives in just about anything. I love this meal because the sauce is done so quickly and has such great flavour.

	Coarse salt
350g	penne
2	tablespoons extra virgin olive oil
2	cloves garlic, peeled and thinly sliced
	Pinch crushed chillies
5	olive oil-packed Spanish anchovies
1	heaped tablespoon salt-packed capers, rinsed
50g	pitted niçoise olives
500ml	Basic Tomato Sauce (page 30)
½	teaspoon freshly ground black pepper, plus more for serving
	A few tablespoons pasta water, to thin
4	tablespoons torn fresh parsley, for garnish

Bring a large saucepan of water to a rolling boil and salt generously. Drop in the penne. Cook according to packet directions.

Meanwhile, put the olive oil in a medium frying pan over medium heat and add the garlic and crushed chillies. Cook for about 1 minute, adjusting the heat if necessary to avoid burning the garlic. Add the anchovies and stir for another minute, or until they begin to break down. Add the capers and olives, crushing them gently with the back of a wooden spoon, and cook for 1 minute, or until quite fragrant – it should smell divine. Stir in the tomato sauce and black pepper. Turn the heat to high, bring to the boil and then reduce heat to medium and let it bubble for about 10 minutes, or until quite thickened. The penne should be perfectly cooked at this point. Drain pasta, reserving a few tablespoons of pasta cooking water. Add pasta to the frying pan with the sauce and stir to coat, adding a bit of the pasta cooking water if necessary to get the sauce to the right consistency. It shouldn't be too thick, but also not too soupy. Scatter the parsley over the pasta, add a bit more fresh black pepper and serve.

make it vegan   Leave out the anchovies.

  SERVES: 4 · ACTIVE & TOTAL PREPARATION TIME: 15 minutes

You can make the sauce ahead of time.

spaghetti limone parmeggiano

AGAIN, EASY PEASY. NOT ONLY CAN this be made while the pasta is cooking, you have plenty of time to make a lovely salad and assemble a cheese plate for after dinner. Parmesan, lemon and basil are a threesome made in heaven. The cheesy lemon basil flavours are also very kid-friendly.

350g	spaghetti
	Coarse salt
1	lemon
100g	Parmesan cheese, finely grated, plus extra for serving
½	teaspoon freshly ground black pepper
2½	tablespoons extra virgin olive oil
3–5	tablespoons of pasta water, to thin
	Handful fresh basil leaves (from 4 leafy stems)

Boil the spaghetti in salted boiling water, according to the packet directions.

Meanwhile, using a Microplane grater, grate the zest from the lemon into a large mixing bowl. Cut the lemon in half and squeeze the juice into the bowl (I like to use the grater as a strainer — one less thing to clean). Add the Parmesan, pepper and a pinch of salt and mix in the olive oil to form a wet paste.

When the spaghetti is perfectly cooked, add 2 or 3 tablespoons of the cooking water to the lemon and cheese mixture. Add the spaghetti to the bowl and toss thoroughly, adding another tablespoon or 2 of pasta water if necessary so that the sauce coats each strand. Roughly tear in the basil leaves.

Serve each portion with a sprinkle of coarse salt, a grind of black pepper and a few gratings of extra Parmesan.

 SERVES: 4 • ACTIVE & TOTAL PREPARATION TIME: 15 minutes

wholewheat pasta with purple sprouting broccoli

SOMETIMES I THINK THAT IF I allowed my children to eat pasta every night, they happily would. Occasionally I try to sneak in the wholewheat variety. It works if the sauce has a lot of flavour, like a garlicky pesto, or this one with anchovy and garlic and purple sprouting broccoli. If you can find it, broccoli rabe is also delish.

	Coarse salt
350g	wholewheat penne or whatever shape you'd like
1	large bunch purple sprouting broccoli
4	tablespoons extra virgin olive oil
4	cloves garlic, peeled and thinly sliced
	Pinch crushed chillies (optional)
6	or 7 olive oil-packed Spanish anchovies
	A few tablespoons pasta water, to thin

Bring a large saucepan of water to a rolling boil and salt generously. Drop in the pasta.

Bring another saucepan of water with a steam basket to the boil. Meanwhile, trim off and discard the bottom portions of the broccoli stems. Steam the broccoli for about 6 minutes, or until just beginning to soften. Drain. Roughly chop it into bite-sized pieces.

Heat the olive oil in a large frying pan over medium-high heat and add the garlic and crushed chillies. Cook for about 30 seconds, adjusting the heat if necessary to avoid burning the garlic. Add the anchovies and stir for another minute, or until they begin to break down. Add the broccoli and sauté for 5–6 minutes, or until just starting to brown.

Drain the pasta and add it to the frying pan with the broccoli, stirring to combine. If it's too dry, add a bit of the pasta water to loosen it.

 SERVES: 4 · ACTIVE & TOTAL PREPARATION TIME: 15 minutes

fried courgette spaghetti

I CAME UP WITH THIS one evening when I was craving two of my favourite things on earth – fried courgettes and, well, spaghetti! The combo is a delight and my kids love it as well. The courgettes get all crispy and sweet.

350g spaghetti

Coarse salt

3 courgettes, very thinly sliced (but thicker than paper thin or they will just burn)

1 tablespoon unbleached plain flour

6 tablespoons extra virgin olive oil

100g Parmesan cheese, finely grated, plus extra for serving

4 tablespoons pasta water, to thin

Freshly ground black pepper

Handful fresh basil leaves (leaves from 5 leafy stems), roughly torn

Boil the spaghetti in salted water until just al dente. Meanwhile, toss the courgettes with the flour. Heat 4 tablespoons of olive oil in a large non-stick frying pan over high heat and add as many courgettes as will fit in a single layer. Cook, stirring and flipping occasionally, until well browned and a little crispy, about 4 minutes. Remove the courgettes to a plate and sprinkle with coarse salt. Repeat until you've cooked all of the courgettes.

Meanwhile, whisk the cheese together with the remaining 2 tablespoons of olive oil in a large mixing bowl. Whisk in 4 tablespoons of the pasta water, adding a bit more if necessary. You want the consistency to be creamy. Drain the spaghetti and add to the bowl with the Parmesan mixture. Toss together, season with salt and pepper and fold in two-thirds of the fried courgettes and all of the basil.

To serve, portion the pasta into four shallow bowls and evenly distribute the rest of the courgettes on top of each, along with a couple of gratings of Parmesan.

 SERVES: 4 • ACTIVE & TOTAL PREPARATION TIME: just shy of ½ hour

turkey bolognese

TWO OF MY PARENTS' CLOSEST FRIENDS are a couple named Robert
and Susan DeLaurentis, who lived down the street from us in Santa Monica.
Robert and my dad made a film together in the 80s and became lifelong pals,
and our families quickly melded together, following suit. Susan is an incredible
home cook and makes one of my favourite dishes in life: her pasta with turkey
sausage and meatballs. She learned the recipe (originally made with veal, pork
and the like) from Robert's Italian *nonna*, and it is a closely guarded family
secret. Susan showed me how to make it, and although I could never expose
her recipe, this one has similar flavours and is made with minced turkey
instead of meatballs. It's a real family crowd pleaser. Maybe one day I'll get
her to give up the secret!

5–6	tablespoons extra virgin olive oil, plus more as needed
350g	Italian turkey sausage, cut into 10cm lengths
450g	minced turkey (ideal to use dark meat)
	Coarse salt
	Freshly ground black pepper
2	medium onions, peeled and finely diced
3	cloves garlic, peeled and finely chopped
4	400g cans whole peeled tomatoes with their juice
5	tablespoons tomato purée
350g	rigatoni
	Grated Parmesan cheese, for serving

Heat 2–3 tablespoons of the olive oil in a large heavy pan over medium-high heat. Add the sausages and cook, turning them now and then, until browned all over, about 10 minutes. Remove the sausages to a plate and add the minced turkey to the pan along with a healthy pinch of salt and a few grinds of pepper. Cook, stirring here and there, for 10 minutes, or until nicely browned. Remove to a separate plate. Add another 2 or 3 tablespoons of olive oil to the pan and add the onion and garlic. Cook these until softened and just beginning to brown, another solid 10 minutes. Add the tomatoes and their juice along with about 125ml of water that you've swished in the cans to get all the tomato out of them. Add the minced turkey, stir the sauce well and nestle the sausages in. Bring the sauce to the boil, season to taste with salt and pepper and turn the heat to low. Cover almost completely with a lid (let the steam escape from one side) and gently simmer for 4 hours (incidentally, this is a great time to use a heat diffuser if you have one), adding splashes of water every hour or so if the sauce is at all drying out. Uncover the sauce and stir in the tomato purée, barely cover, and simmer for 1 more hour.

When it's about ready for serving, bring a large saucepan of water to a rolling boil and salt generously. Drop the rigatoni in and cook according to packet directions.

Serve the sauce over the cooked rigatoni with a nice grating of Parmesan on top. Perfect.

SERVES: 4 with enough for leftovers · ACTIVE PREPARATION TIME: 40 minutes
TOTAL PREPARATION TIME: 5 hours

sweet potato ravioli

MAKING RAVIOLI IS A PERFECT SUNDAY project. Kids love getting in there and helping with all of the steps. I always make lots more to freeze – it's a brilliant thing to have to hand for a day when you are short on time and you want a quick, elegant dinner. This recipe calls for a sweet potato filling, but you can do anything you like: puréed spinach with mascarpone, peas and ricotta – it's a great way to get healthy veggies in.

for the pasta

- 1 recipe Fresh Pasta (page 123), in 7.5cm-wide sheets

for the filling

- 1 sweet potato, peeled and cut into 8 pieces
- 4 tablespoons finely grated Parmesan cheese
- 2 tablespoons mascarpone

  Coarse salt

  Freshly ground black pepper

  Freshly grated nutmeg
- 1 organic large egg white, beaten

for finishing

50g unsalted butter

- 6 fresh large sage leaves, thinly sliced

  Grated Parmesan cheese, for serving

For the pasta, keep the dough sheets covered with a tea towel or clingfilm while you prepare the filling.

For the filling, steam the sweet potato pieces for 20 minutes, or until cooked through. Mash the sweet potato in a bowl and stir in the cheeses. Season the mixture generously with salt and cautiously with pepper and nutmeg, tasting along the way. Let the mixture cool before proceeding.

To assemble the ravioli, dollop teaspoons of the filling along half the pasta sheets, leaving 5cm between each spoonful. Using a pastry brush, brush the egg white along the tops and bottoms of the pasta sheets that you've placed filling on and brush between each dollop of filling. Lay the untouched pasta sheets over the filled ones. Using your fingers, seal the edges around each bit of filling, pushing out the air as best you can. Using a paring knife, cut the ravioli into squares. Trim away any extra pasta so that you are left with uniform, neat ravioli. Using your fingers, pinch each ravioli's edges to be sure that they're sealed.

For finishing the ravioli, bring a large saucepan of salted water to the boil. Cook the ravioli in batches for 2½ minutes, and remove them with a large perforated spoon to warmed plates. Meanwhile, melt the butter with the sage in a small saucepan over low heat. Spoon the butter over the ravioli, evenly distributing the sage. Scatter as much Parmesan as you'd like over each portion and serve.

 SERVES: 8 • ACTIVE PREPARATION TIME: 1 hour • TOTAL PREPARATION TIME: 1½ hours

artichoke & pine nut pesto

THIS SIMPLE PESTO IS GOOD with spaghetti or you can serve it as a spread
– grill some good country bread and spread it on.

175g	cooked artichoke hearts
2	tablespoons raw pine nuts
4	tablespoons extra virgin olive oil
1	small clove garlic, peeled and finely chopped
30g	Parmesan cheese, finely grated
	Pinch coarse salt
	A few grinds of black pepper
2	teaspoons fresh tarragon leaves, thinly sliced
2–3	teaspoons pasta water, to thin

Pulse the first 7 ingredients together in a food processor. Stir in the tarragon and season to taste with more salt and pepper if needed. When you're serving it, it's good to loosen the mixture with a little pasta cooking water.

 SERVES: 4 • **ACTIVE & TOTAL PREPARATION TIME: 10 minutes**

cavolo nero pesto with penne & peas

THIS PESTO IS PERFECT in the winter, when cavolo nero, which is a dark green leafy vegetable that's very good for you, is in season.

1	bunch cavolo nero or your favourite hearty winter greens
10	olive oil-packed Spanish anchovies
1	small clove garlic, peeled and finely chopped
5	tablespoons extra virgin olive oil
	Freshly ground black pepper
80g	mascarpone
350g	penne rigate
150g	frozen peas
	Freshly grated Parmesan cheese, for serving
1	teacup pasta water, to thin

Steam the cavolo nero for 7 minutes. Whizz it together with the anchovies, garlic, olive oil and pepper in a blender until just smooth. Pour into a bowl and stir in the mascarpone.

Meanwhile, cook the penne according to the packet directions, adding the peas during the last 3 minutes of cooking. Reserving a teacup of the cooking water, drain the pasta and peas and combine them with the pesto, thinning with a bit of the water if necessary. Serve with plenty of Parmesan.

 SERVES: 4 • **ACTIVE & TOTAL PREPARATION TIME: 15 minutes**

duck ragu

ONE YEAR I WAS GIVEN a birthday present I'll never forget – a cooking lesson from Jamie Oliver. He came over and showed me how to make one of my favourite and most sentimental dishes – duck ragu. His recipe had more of a Moroccan bent with raisins and oranges, and it was magical. Over the years the recipe has become its own thing in my kitchen, but the roasting technique is all Jamie. I think this may just be my favourite recipe in the whole book. The gremolata topping, while optional, takes it to another level.

1	organic large duck, washed and dried (See Salt Scrubs for Poultry, page 43)
3	tablespoons extra virgin olive oil
	Coarse salt
	Freshly ground black pepper
4	slices duck bacon (or whatever bacon you love), finely diced
1	medium onion, peeled and finely diced
2	medium carrots, peeled and finely diced
2	medium stalks celery, finely diced
5	cloves garlic, peeled and minced
2	12.5cm sprigs fresh rosemary, stems discarded and leaves finely chopped
3	400g cans whole peeled tomatoes with their juice
250ml	Italian red wine
100ml	tomato purée
450g	pappardelle (fresh or dried)
	Gremolata Breadcrumbs (page 139) or freshly grated Parmesan cheese, for serving

Preheat the oven to 180°C (350°F) gas 4.

Trim off excess skin from the opening to the duck's cavity and from the back end. Rub the entire duck with 1 tablespoon of olive oil and sprinkle liberally with salt and pepper, inside and out. Roast it for a total of 2 hours, flipping it from its back to its breast (and vice versa) every ½ hour. Let it cool in the pan until you can handle it. Drain off the fat and either discard it or reserve for another use, such as roasting potatoes.

While the duck is roasting, heat 2 tablespoons of olive oil in a casserole over medium-high heat and add the bacon. Cook for 5 minutes, stirring occasionally, or until starting to crisp. Add the onion, carrots, celery, garlic and rosemary, turn the heat down to low, and cook, stirring occasionally, for 15 minutes, or until softened. Add the tomatoes and their juice and put 125ml water into one can, swish it around to get all the tomato stuck to the sides, pour into the next can and repeat again with the third. Add the tomato water to the casserole along with the wine, a good grind of pepper and a healthy pinch of salt. Bring to the boil and then turn the heat down very low and let simmer for 1 hour 15 minutes.

After the duck has cooled down a bit, remove and discard the skin and bones and shred the meat. Fold the duck meat into the ragu along with the tomato purée and cook on very low heat, uncovered, for at least 1 hour and up to 4, adding splashes of water if necessary to keep it from drying out (continue to season with salt and pepper as you splash).

To serve, cook the pasta, divide it between bowls, and spoon a generous amount of duck ragu over the pasta. Top with the Gremolata Breadcrumbs or Parmesan.

 SERVES: 4–6 • ACTIVE PREPARATION TIME: 50 minutes • TOTAL PREPARATION TIME: 4–5 hours

gremolata breadcrumbs

35g fresh breadcrumbs, toasted and coarsely ground

Zest of 2 lemons

1½ tablespoons finely chopped fresh parsley

Small pinch of coarse salt

Toss everything together.

 YIELD: 250ml • **ACTIVE & TOTAL PREPARATION TIME:** less than 5 minutes

macaroni cheese (a few ways)

I GREW UP LOOKING FORWARD to the nights we had 'mac and cheese'; my mother would pop the supermarket frozen kind in the toaster oven and the bubbling American cheese would go all brown on top. My brother and I used to fight over the crispy bits. In this more Italian-leaning (and preservative-free) version, the ultimate comfort food gets an elegant makeover. I love to serve this in ramekins for individual portions, adjusting the flavours at the end for each member of my family.

450g	macaroni (preferably with ridges)
225g	mascarpone
	Pinch freshly grated nutmeg
100g	Parmesan cheese, grated, plus 50g for topping
125ml	milk
	Coarse salt
	Freshly ground black pepper
50g	dry breadcrumbs
25g	unsalted butter

for variation add one of the following:

250ml	Basic Tomato Sauce (page 30)
1	ball fresh mozzarella, cubed
50g	Gorgonzola cheese, crumbled
50g	Taleggio cheese, broken into small pieces

Preheat the oven to 200°C (400°F) gas 6 and turn it on to fan heat if that's a possibility.

In a large saucepan of boiling salted water, cook the macaroni for 2 minutes less than indicated on the packet. Meanwhile, stir together the mascarpone, nutmeg and 100g Parmesan in a small saucepan over a medium heat until the cheeses melt together, about 2 minutes. Stir in the milk and salt and pepper to taste and keep the sauce warm over a low heat. Drain the pasta and combine it with the sauce.

In a small bowl, stir together the remaining 50g Parmesan and the breadcrumbs. At this point, you can put the macaroni in a large baking dish, scatter the breadcrumb topping over it, dot it with the butter and bake it for 15 minutes and it will be great.

Or you can do any of the following variations, which can be done in mini ramekins to make individual servings:

1 Put a layer of tomato sauce on the bottom of the baking dish, then pour the macaroni over the sauce, sprinkle with the breadcrumb mixture, dot with butter and bake for 15 minutes.

2 Mix the mozzarella with the macaroni before pouring into the baking dish. Top with the breadcrumb mixture, dot with butter and bake for 15 minutes. This is also particularly nice with the tomato sauce base as in number 1, above.

3 After you pour the macaroni into the baking dish, tuck in tiny bits of the crumbled Gorgonzola, sprinkle with the breadcrumb mixture, dot with butter and bake for 15 minutes.

4 After you pour the macaroni into the baking dish, put a layer of Taleggio on top, sprinkle with the breadcrumb mixture, dot with butter and bake for 15 minutes.

 SERVES: 4 · ACTIVE PREPARATION TIME: 20 minutes · TOTAL PREPARATION TIME: 35 minutes

 The macaroni cheese can be made up to the point of baking way in advance.

cacio e pepe

THIS IS ONE OF THOSE DISHES I like to make when I want a meal that is done in the time it takes to cook pasta. When my kids were babies with an early bedtime (before we all started eating together early), I would cut this recipe down and have a quick, cosy meal with a big glass of wine.

350g	spaghetti
	Coarse salt
2	tablespoons your best, highest-quality olive oil
40g	Parmesan cheese, finely grated
40g	pecorino cheese, finely grated
	Freshly ground black pepper
1	teacup pasta water, to thin

Cook the spaghetti in a large saucepan of salted water until perfectly al dente. Meanwhile, combine the oil, cheeses and lots of pepper in a large bowl. Drain the spaghetti, reserving a teacup of pasta water, and add about 4 tablespoons of the pasta water to the cheese mixture. Stir to combine and then add the spaghetti, thinning with a little pasta water only if necessary so that the spaghetti is evenly coated with sauce (there should be just enough sauce to coat it without any excess). Serve each portion with a pinch of coarse salt on top.

 SERVES: 4 • **ACTIVE & TOTAL PREPARATION TIME: 15 minutes**

rocket & tomato pasta

THE ROCKET THROWN IN at the end gives this pasta dish a bright green addition of flavour and texture and beautifully contrasts the sweet sauce. I originally got this idea from *The River Cafe Cookbook Green*. I like to make this in the summer and serve it with tagliatelle.

2	tablespoons extra virgin olive oil
4	cloves garlic, peeled and thinly sliced
¼	teaspoon crushed chillies
1	teaspoon fennel seeds, crushed with a mallet or pestle and mortar
3	400g cans whole peeled tomatoes with their juice
	Coarse salt
	Freshly ground black pepper
350g	spaghetti, tagliatelle or Fresh Pasta (page 23)
75g	rocket (3 large handfuls)
	Grated Parmesan cheese, for serving

Heat the olive oil in a large saucepan over medium-low heat, add the garlic, crushed chillies, and fennel, and cook, stirring, for 3 minutes, or until very fragrant. Add the tomatoes and their juice, season with salt and pepper, turn the heat to high and bring the sauce to the boil. Turn the heat to medium-low and let the sauce cook on a low boil for 1 hour.

About 10 minutes before you're ready to eat, boil the spaghetti in salted boiling water. A minute before it's al dente, add the rocket to the pasta pan. Drain the pasta and rocket and toss them with the tomato sauce.

Serve each portion with plenty of grated Parmesan.

SERVES: 4 • ACTIVE PREPARATION TIME: 15 minutes
TOTAL PREPARATION TIME: 1 hour and 15 minutes

main
courses

Around the time my son turned three and a half, we started having early family dinners all together and it quickly became one of the best parts of my life. The meal, acting as a way to bring us all together and hear each other out, is the highlight of my day. I never could have anticipated the genuinely interesting and hilarious insights that would come out of the mouths of the kids, or just the general feeling of closeness and happiness. The other night, my daughter turned to my son and said, 'When we get older, we'll eat dinner together, right?' This comment made me realize how important these family meals are to my children too. The food can be as simple as can be, even a Chinese takeaway – just all of us sitting together without television, BlackBerrys, and the like, is gold. Sometimes we can't pull it off because life gets in the way, but when we can, I always feel tremendous gratitude.

These tried and tested main courses have come out of my kitchen many, many times. We like it simple, we like it rustic, we like it delectable, and, above all, we like it to say home. Some are super simple, some require a bit of time, but none will fail you. There are two basic family-friendly categories here that most of the dishes fit into – the prepare-ahead option and the quick and delish option.

chicken milanese: four very special ways

CHICKEN MILANESE IS ONE of the most simple, most satisfying dishes. I like to cut my son's chicken into strips and shallow-fry them, squeezing on a bit of lemon at the end for good measure. The four topping options on the following pages are as easy as they are diverse – choose according to your tastes. If you are entertaining a group, you can make all four and serve them in the middle of the table – your guests can choose.

4	skinless, free-range, organic boneless chicken breasts, washed and dried (See Salt Scrubs for Poultry, page 43)
250ml	milk
200g	dry breadcrumbs (Japanese panko makes the crispiest crust) mixed with 1 teaspoon freshly ground pepper and 1 teaspoon coarse salt
125ml	extra virgin olive oil

Place the chicken breasts between two pieces of baking paper. Using a mallet, pound the chicken breasts until they're very, very thin – you should be able to almost see through them – about 1.5mm thick. Put the milk in a shallow bowl and the breadcrumbs on a large plate. Dip each piece of chicken into the milk and then dredge it in the breadcrumbs, tapping off the excess. You should have a thin, even coating.

Heat half the olive oil in a large non-stick frying pan big enough to hold 2 pieces of the chicken in a single layer. Cook for about 4 minutes on the first side, or until evenly browned and crisp. Flip and cook for an additional 2 or 3 minutes, or until the other side is browned and crisp and the chicken is firm to the touch. Wipe out the pan and repeat with the remaining olive oil and the remaining 2 pieces of chicken.

Proceed with one of the four variations on pages 148 and 149.

note: You can also remove the flaps of meat from the undersides of the chicken breasts and make 'Mini-Milanese' for the kids.

 SERVES: 4 · ACTIVE & TOTAL PREPARATION TIME: ½ hour for the chicken plus time for each topping

OPPOSITE: Chicken Milanese with Slow-Roasted Cherry Tomatoes & Rocket

SLOW-ROASTED CHERRY TOMATOES & ROCKET

450g   cherry tomatoes
  2   tablespoons extra virgin olive oil
      Coarse salt
 75g   wild rocket
  1   tablespoon high-quality balsamic vinegar

ONE OF MY BEST FRIENDS once called me in a panic – she had to cook dinner for her boyfriend and did not know what to make – she had never cooked anything. I described how to prepare the Chicken Milanese and winged this topping – it was a hit. She, and I, make it to this day.

Preheat the oven to 200°C (400°F) gas 6.

Place the tomatoes in a small baking tin and drizzle with 1 tablespoon of the olive oil and a pinch of salt. Roast for 45 minutes, stirring occasionally, until they're split and blistered and super sweet.

While the chicken is cooking, toss the rocket with the remaining tablespoon of olive oil, the vinegar and a pinch of salt. Fold the tomatoes into the rocket.

Place one piece of chicken on each of four dinner plates and mound a handful of rocket over each piece, making sure everyone gets plenty of tomatoes.

note: It's nice to mix ½ teaspoon of dried oregano into the breadcrumbs of the Chicken Milanese recipe for this version.

ACTIVE PREPARATION TIME: 5 minutes (For quicker preparation time, the roasted cherry tomatoes can be made ahead.) • TOTAL PREPARATION TIME: 50 minutes

CHICORY & GORGONZOLA

  2   tablespoons extra virgin olive oil
  2   large heads chicory, roughly chopped into 1cm-wide pieces
 50g   Gorgonzola cheese, crumbled

THIS TOPPING IS OUT of this world – I would serve it as a side dish with steak if I ate steak. The bitterness of the chicory gives way to its hidden sweetness as it cooks and the Gorgonzola . . . well, need I say more.

Heat the olive oil in a medium frying pan over medium-high heat. Add the chicory and sauté for 5–7 minutes, or until browned and softened. Pull off the heat and stir in the Gorgonzola.

Place one piece of chicken on each of four dinner plates and divide the chicory and Gorgonzola mixture over each piece.

ACTIVE & TOTAL PREPARATION TIME: 10 minutes

MANY HERB SALAD & DRIED CRANBERRIES

1 tablespoon extra virgin olive oil

4 tablespoons roughly chopped fresh chives

4 tablespoons roughly chopped fresh coriander

2 tablespoons roughly chopped fresh flat-leaf parsley

1 tablespoon finely chopped fresh mint

2 tablespoons dried cranberries

Juice of ½ lemon

Coarse salt

I CAME UP WITH THIS near Thanksgiving one year when I had cranberries on my mind. It would also be really good sprinkled with feta or goat's cheese.

Combine the olive oil, herbs, cranberries and lemon juice together in a small bowl and season with salt.

Place one piece of chicken on each of four dinner plates and divide the herb salad over each piece.

ACTIVE & TOTAL PREPARATION TIME: 10 minutes

TOMATO & AVOCADO SALAD

1 avocado, peeled, stoned and roughly chopped

225g cherry tomatoes, quartered

4 tablespoons roughly chopped spring onions or red onion

1 tablespoon roughly chopped coriander leaves

1 tablespoon extra virgin olive oil

2 limes

I LIKE THIS VERSION in the summer. For extra taste, add a teaspoon of ground coriander into the breadcrumb mixture.

Combine the avocado, tomatoes, spring onions and coriander in a bowl. Dress with the olive oil and the juice of 1 lime.

Place one piece of chicken on each of four dinner plates and divide the salad over each piece. Quarter the remaining lime and put a piece on each plate for each person to squeeze over the food.

ACTIVE & TOTAL PREPARATION TIME: 10 minutes

indian-spiced tuna steaks

A GRILLED TUNA STEAK with a twist. I love this Indian-inspired spice rub – it definitely livens things up. Served with Raita and Tamarind Chutney, the flavours are complex enough to make things interesting while making kids happy.

2 teaspoons cumin seeds

2 teaspoons fennel seeds

1 teaspoon coarse salt

1 teaspoon freshly ground black pepper

2 tablespoons peeled and finely chopped fresh ginger

4 tablespoons fresh coriander leaves

4 tablespoons extra virgin olive oil

4 tuna steaks, each about 2cm thick

Raita (page 151)

Tamarind Chutney (page 151)

Combine the cumin and fennel seeds with the salt and pepper and crush them using a pestle and mortar, coffee grinder or Jamie Oliver's ingenious Flavour Shaker until the seeds are broken but not powdery. Add the ginger and coriander and crush until a rough paste begins to form. Stir in the olive oil. The mixture should be a bit like pesto. Rub the tuna steaks all over with the mixture and let them sit in the refrigerator for at least 2 hours, or up to overnight if you wish.

Preheat the barbecue or a griddle pan over high heat.

Grill the tuna steaks for about 2 minutes on the first side, or until a spatula slides easily under a steak and the bottom half of it has turned opaque. Flip each steak and cook for an additional minute. Serve with Raita and Tamarind Chutney.

SERVES: 4 • ACTIVE PREPARATION TIME: 20 minutes
TOTAL PREPARATION TIME: 20 minutes plus at least 2 hours marinating

raita

½ large cucumber, peeled, seeds removed, finely diced

2 tablespoons peeled and finely chopped red onion

1 tablespoon finely sliced fresh mint

125ml natural yogurt

A few grinds black pepper

Combine all the ingredients in a bowl and stir. Serve with the Indian-Spiced Tuna Steaks.

 YIELD: 250ml • ACTIVE & TOTAL PREPARATION TIME: 10 minutes

tamarind chutney

1 tablespoon vegetable oil

1 teaspoon cumin seeds

1 teaspoon fennel seeds

⅛–¼ teaspoon cayenne pepper (optional, depending on how spicy you like things – ¼ teaspoon has a lot of heat)

1 teaspoon ground ginger

1 generous teaspoon garam masala

Tiny pinch asafoetida (optional)

250ml water

1 tablespoon tamarind paste

4 tablespoons unrefined dark brown sugar

2 teaspoons rice wine vinegar

Heat the vegetable oil in a frying pan over medium heat. Add the cumin and fennel seeds and stir for 30 seconds. Add the remaining spices and cook, stirring, for a minute. Add the water, tamarind and sugar and stir or whisk until smooth. Simmer on low for 25 minutes and then stir in the vinegar. Bring it up to the boil, lower the heat and simmer for another 10–15 minutes, until the sauce has reduced to a slightly thicker consistency.

note: You can lessen the amount of or leave out the cayenne if you are making it for the kids, but they like the sweetness of this chutney.

 YIELD: 125ml • ACTIVE PREPARATION TIME: 10 minutes
TOTAL PREPARATION TIME: 45 minutes

roast chicken, rotisserie style

I GREW UP HAVING AMERICAN rotisserie chicken at the Brentwood Country Mart in Los Angeles – nothing can beat that place. Still, this version helps bring me back to my childhood. Here, as opposed to putting chicken on a turning spit, you rotate the chicken and it self-bastes. I read about this technique in a Joël Robuchon cookbook and adapted it to have an American rotisserie flavour.

20g unsalted butter, room temperature

¾ teaspoon garlic salt

¾ teaspoon sweet paprika

¼ teaspoon freshly ground black pepper

Coarse salt

1 organic whole chicken (1.4–1.8kg), washed and dried (See Salt Scrubs for Poultry, page 43)

Preheat the oven (preferably a fan oven) to 200°C (400°F) gas 6.

Mix the butter together with the garlic salt, paprika, pepper and a very large pinch of coarse salt. Gently separate the skin from the breast by inserting your fingers between the skin and breast and breaking the soft connective tissue. This will lead to crispier skin. Rub the butter all over the chicken, including a bit between the breast and the skin. Tuck the wings underneath the bird and tie one piece of kitchen string around them to secure them. Tie the legs together with another piece of kitchen string.

Put the chicken on its side (resting on its thigh and wing) in a large heavy roasting tin and roast for 25 minutes. Turn it onto its other side and sprinkle with a few tablespoons of water. Return the chicken to the oven and roast for an additional 25 minutes. Turn it on its back and roast for 10 minutes. Turn it onto its breast and roast for 10 minutes. Remove the chicken from the oven and let it rest breast side down for at least 15 minutes. Carve and serve.

SERVES: 4 · ACTIVE PREPARATION TIME: 15 minutes · TOTAL PREPARATION TIME: 1½ hours

whole roasted fish
with salsa verde

THIS IS AN OLD DINNER party standby – it's super simple and incredibly delicious and is basically foolproof. Served on the bone, it is full of flavour and moisture. I love it with salsa verde, but you can also just dress it with great olive oil and a squeeze of lemon.

1 very fresh whole sea bass or whatever fish is good, fresh, and preferably local (at least 900g), scaled and gutted

1 tablespoon each fresh tarragon, basil, chives and parsley

1 lemon, cut into thin slices

2 tablespoons extra virgin olive oil

Freshly ground black pepper

Coarse salt

Salsa Verde (page 156), for serving

Preheat the oven to 220°C (425°F) gas 7.

Cut 4 or 5 slits on each side of the fish, about 1cm into the flesh. Combine the herbs and roughly chop them. Stuff each opening with a slice of lemon and a little bit of the herb mixture. Put any remaining herbs and lemon slices in the cavity of the fish. Lay the fish in a large roasting tin. Drizzle with the olive oil and sprinkle with black pepper and salt. Roast for 30–40 minutes, or until the fish is firm but still moist.

To serve, gently spoon the top fillet off the bone. You can then easily peel the bones off in one piece from the bottom half. Serve with plenty of Salsa Verde.

SERVES: 4 • ACTIVE PREPARATION TIME: 10 minutes • TOTAL PREPARATION TIME: 45 minutes
The dressed fish can sit in the fridge for a few hours.

salsa verde

THIS IS A HARD RECIPE to write down precisely. My measurements are always a little different and my herbs change frequently, depending on what's growing in my garden and what I'm serving it with. This is my standard salsa verde – heavy on the chives, easy on the parsley, generous, as always, with the anchovies.

6 olive oil-packed Spanish anchovies

1 generous teaspoon Dijon mustard

1 tablespoon red wine vinegar

4 tablespoons roughly chopped fresh parsley

5 tablespoons roughly chopped fresh basil

5 tablespoons roughly chopped fresh coriander

8 tablespoons roughly chopped fresh chives

4 tablespoons extra virgin olive oil

Freshly ground black pepper

Put the anchovies in a bowl and cut into small pieces with a knife and fork (this saves you a board to wash!). Stir in the mustard and vinegar. Add the herbs, slowly stream in the olive oil and season with pepper.

 YIELD: 125ml • ACTIVE & TOTAL PREPARATION TIME: 10 minutes

 Can be made ahead, but it must be eaten on the same day.

best stir-fried chicken

THIS IS A GREAT FAST MAIN COURSE. I love making this when I'm in the mood
for good Chinese takeaway but don't want to have the MSG. Ready in minutes,
it's a real family pleaser – the caramelized, sweet chicken goes down like a treat.

4	skinless, boneless chicken breasts, cut into small (about 2cm) cubes
2	tablespoons cornflour
	Coarse salt
	Freshly ground black pepper
2	tablespoons vegetable oil
4	tablespoons peeled and finely chopped garlic
4	tablespoons peeled and finely chopped ginger
4	large spring onions, finely sliced (white and green parts)
	Pinch crushed chillies (optional)
125ml	rice wine vinegar
125g	dark brown sugar (unrefined if possible)
2	tablespoons soy sauce
2	tablespoons coarsely chopped fresh coriander, for serving

Toss the chicken with the cornflour, a large pinch of salt and quite a bit of
pepper. Heat the oil in a large non-stick wok over medium-high heat (this is
a gentle stir-fry). Add the garlic, ginger, spring onions, and crushed chillies,
if using them, and cook, stirring, for 1 minute. Add the chicken and cook,
stirring occasionally, for 5 minutes. Add the vinegar, sugar and 5 or 6 grinds
of black pepper. Boil on high for 3 minutes, or until the sugar has really
caramelized, the vinegar has mellowed a bit and the whole mixture is dark
brown and sticky and lovely. Add the soy sauce, cook for another 30 seconds
and serve immediately, sprinkled with the coriander.

note: It's especially good with the Fried Rice with Kale & Spring Onions
(page 198).

make it vegan   Replace the chicken with similar amounts of
tofu or simply vegetables.

  SERVES: 4 • ACTIVE & TOTAL PREPARATION TIME: 15 minutes

chicken & dumplings

THIS IS PROBABLY THE HOMIEST dish in the book. I absolutely love to make this; it's an uncomplicated one-pot dish that you can prepare in the morning and keep on the back of the stove, building deep layers of flavour. The chicken falls off the bone and the scone-like dumplings are light and delicious. I was seven when my mother filmed *The Great Santini* in Beaufort, South Carolina – one of the happiest times in my childhood. I spent afternoons running around the marshes and would come home to freshly baked scones by Neetha Polite, the lady who was looking after us. The dumplings in the recipe are inspired by her. When I make this, it vanishes – there are never any leftovers.

1	organic whole chicken
	Coarse salt
	Freshly ground black pepper
15g	unsalted butter
2	tablespoons extra virgin olive oil
1	stalk celery, roughly chopped
1	large carrot, peeled and roughly chopped
1	small leek, roughly chopped
1	slice duck bacon (or whatever bacon you love), finely diced
1	dried bay leaf
1	teaspoon fresh thyme leaves
125ml	white wine
500ml	Vegetable Stock (page 36) or Chicken Stock (page 39)
500ml	water
125g	unbleached plain or white spelt flour
1	tablespoon baking powder
125ml	single cream
½	teaspoon fine salt
	Fresh parsley, for garnish

Preheat the oven to 200°C (400°F) gas 6.

Wash and dry the chicken (See Salt Scrubs for Poultry, page 43). Discard the back and cut the chicken into 10 pieces.

Aggressively season the chicken pieces with coarse salt and pepper. Heat the butter and olive oil in the largest, widest ovenproof pan you have (at least 30cm in diameter, with a lid) over medium-high heat. Thoroughly brown the chicken pieces, in batches if necessary (7–8 minutes per side), and remove to a plate, leaving the fat in the pan. Add the vegetables, bacon, bay leaf and thyme to the pan and cook for 15 minutes over medium-low heat. Return the chicken to the pan. Add the white wine, bring to the boil and cook for 2 minutes. Add the stock and water, bring to the boil and season to taste with salt and pepper. Turn off the heat, cover the pan with a circle of baking paper, and put the lid on top. Cook the chicken in the preheated oven for 1½ hours.

Meanwhile, combine the flour, baking powder, cream and fine salt together in a bowl. Take the pan out of the oven, discard the paper and scoop large spoonfuls of the dumpling mixture on top of the chicken mixture – you should end up with about 10 dumplings. Cover the pan and put back in the oven for 10 minutes. Sprinkle with parsley and a bit more ground black pepper. Serve immediately, being sure to spoon plenty of the juices over each portion.

 SERVES: 4 · ACTIVE PREPARATION TIME: 1 hour
TOTAL PREPARATION TIME: 2½ hours

 This can be made ahead up until the point of the dumplings.

fried flounder or plaice with tartar sauce

WHILE I WAS GROWING UP my mom had a few dinner specialities in high rotation. This was my favourite of the bunch – crispy fried flounder. She used to serve it with Stouffer's macaroni and cheese, which I've omitted here (but you could try the Macaroni Cheese recipe on page 141 to go with it if you want). To this day, fried flounder says home to me. My kids love it just as much as I do.

4	large flounder or plaice, or any flat white fish fillets
125ml	milk
200g	fine dry breadcrumbs
	Safflower or groundnut oil, for frying
	Fine salt
1	lemon, cut into wedges, for serving
	Tartar Sauce (recipe follows), for serving

Dip the fish in the milk and then lightly dredge in breadcrumbs. Place a large non-stick frying pan over medium-high heat and fill with 5mm of safflower oil (about 175ml). When a small pinch of breadcrumbs sizzles immediately, gently lay the fish in the pan (do this in batches if necessary). Fry for about 3 minutes per side, or until golden brown and crispy. Drain on kitchen paper and sprinkle with a pinch of salt. Serve with lemon wedges and tartar sauce.

make it kid friendly Cut the fillets into fish fingers before frying for the kids.

 SERVES: 4 • ACTIVE & TOTAL PREPARATION TIME: 15 minutes

tartar sauce

300ml	Vegenaise or mayo
3	tablespoons salt-packed capers, rinsed and drained
4	tablespoons cornichons, very finely chopped
4	tablespoons fresh basil leaves, finely chopped
2	tablespoons finely chopped fresh chives
1	teaspoon lemon juice
¼	teaspoon freshly ground black pepper

Stir everything together.

 YIELD: 325ml
ACTIVE & TOTAL PREPARATION TIME: 10 minutes

salmon with ginger conserve & thyme

THIS WAS A BRUCE PALTROW summer barbecue special. He had a big Weber grill that sat on an expansive wooden deck overlooking Lake Waccabuc. Taking great pleasure in firing it up, he was very specific about his smoked wood chips and the charcoal he used to get the fire going ('No lighter fluid, it ruins the taste!'). The ginger conserve caramelizes on the salmon – it's got a sweet, smoky flavour on the barbecue. I like to grill slices of oil-brushed onions to serve on the side.

4	175g salmon fillets (with the skin on)
	Coarse salt
	Freshly ground black pepper
8	tablespoons ginger conserve (I like the Wilkin & Sons brand.)
1	tablespoon fresh thyme leaves

Heat the barbecue to medium-high heat.

Sprinkle each piece of salmon with salt and pepper and then evenly distribute the ginger conserve, being sure to coat not only the tops of the fillets but also the sides. Sprinkle the top of each fillet with the thyme leaves.

Place the salmon skin side down on the barbecue, cover and cook for 10 minutes. Slide a large, sturdy spatula in between the skin and the flesh of each fillet and carefully lift the fillets off the skin – this should happen pretty easily. Discard the salmon skin.

 SERVES: 4 • ACTIVE PREPARATION TIME: 5 minutes • TOTAL PREPARATION TIME: 15 minutes

sole à la grenobloise

ONE EVENING OUT AT THE BEACH my mother invited some of her friends over and I was assigned chef duties with not a lot of time to prepare. I made this flavourful, light sautéed fish, based on the classic French preparation. I didn't let her down! The browned butter and fresh lemon are the perfect complement for white flaky sole.

125ml	milk
125g	unbleached plain flour seasoned with a large pinch of salt and a few grinds of black pepper
4	fillets of sole, skin removed (each should weigh about 125g)
4	tablespoons extra virgin olive oil
50g	unsalted butter
2	tablespoons salt-packed capers, rinsed and drained
1	lemon, skin and pith discarded, cut into thin circles
	Maldon sea salt

Put the milk and flour in separate shallow bowls. Dip the fillets in the milk and then lightly dredge in the flour. Heat the olive oil and half the butter in a large non-stick frying pan over medium-high heat. Gently lay the fillets down in the pan and cook for 2 minutes on each side, or until cooked through and nicely golden brown. Do this in batches if necessary.

While the fish is cooking, heat the remaining butter in a small saucepan over medium-high heat. When it's just beginning to brown and the surface is foamy, about 1½ minutes, swirl in the capers and remove from the heat. Add the lemon circles.

Transfer the fish fillets to a serving plate, spoon over the sauce, being sure to evenly distribute the capers and lemon. Sprinkle each fillet with a bit of coarse salt and serve.

 SERVES: 4 • ACTIVE & TOTAL PREPARATION TIME: 20 minutes

fish tacos

THE PERFECT FAMILY MEAL! I like to put the various accoutrements in little bowls so that everyone can assemble their own taco – it becomes a fun, creative project, and a delicious one at that. My veggie daughter omits the fish and has black beans in her tortilla with the salsa and guacamole.

To make it a healthier option, marinate the fish in olive oil, lots of lime juice, salt, pepper and roughly chopped coriander (optional) for at least an hour and up to overnight. Grill the fish for a few minutes per side, depending on the thickness.

	Safflower or groundnut oil, for frying
125g	unbleached plain flour
250ml	beer
	Coarse salt
¼	teaspoon freshly ground pepper
675g	white fish fillets (cod, pollock and haddock are all good choices – whatever's best that day), cut into finger-sized pieces (about 5cm long and 1cm thick)
	Corn tortillas
	Lime Crema (page 167)
	Pico de Gallo (page 166)
	Salted Cabbage (page 166)
	Guacamole (page 166)
	Cholula hot sauce

Pour 5cm of safflower oil into a large saucepan or fill your deep-fat fryer. Heat to 175°C (350°F).

Meanwhile, combine the flour, beer, a pinch of salt and the pepper together in a large bowl. Dredge the fish in the batter and gently place in the hot oil, being careful not to crowd the pan. Fry for 3–4 minutes, turning here and there, until nicely browned. Remove to a kitchen-paper-lined plate, sprinkle with a little salt and repeat with as many batches as necessary until you've cooked all your fish.

To serve, warm the corn tortillas on both sides in a frying pan with just a bit of oil or butter. Serve a stack of them alongside all your fillings. To assemble, spread a spoonful of lime crema on a tortilla, lay 2 or 3 pieces of fried fish on top, scatter generously with pico de gallo, a bit of salted cabbage and some guacamole. I like mine with some hot sauce too.

 SERVES: 4 • ACTIVE & TOTAL PREPARATION TIME: 25 minutes

pico de gallo

225g cherry tomatoes, quartered

½ small red onion, peeled and very finely diced

2 tablespoons finely chopped fresh coriander

Maldon sea salt

1 lime

Combine the tomatoes, onion and coriander in a bowl. Season to taste with salt and lime juice.

  YIELD: 500ml • ACTIVE & TOTAL PREPARATION TIME: 10 minutes

salted cabbage

½ very small green cabbage, coarsely grated

Juice of ½ lime

Pinch Maldon sea salt

Combine everything together and let it sit for 20 minutes. The cabbage will wilt slightly, but will retain its crunch.

  YIELD: 250ml • ACTIVE PREPARATION TIME: 5 minutes
TOTAL PREPARATION TIME: 25 minutes

guacamole

2 ripe avocados

2 tablespoons peeled and finely chopped onion

3 tablespoons roughly chopped fresh coriander

1 lime

Coarse salt

Cut the avocados in half, remove and reserve the stones, and score the flesh inside the shells. Scoop the avocado into a mixing bowl and mash gently with a fork – you don't want it to be completely smooth. Stir in the onion and coriander. Cut the lime in half and squeeze in enough juice to taste. Season the guacamole with salt and either serve immediately or stick the stones in to keep it from browning (remove the stones before serving).

  YIELD: 375ml • ACTIVE & TOTAL PREPARATION TIME: 10 minutes

lime crema

125ml	Vegenaise or mayo
1	tablespoon fresh lime juice
	Coarse salt

Stir together the Vegenaise and lime juice and season with salt.

 YIELD: 125ml • ACTIVE & TOTAL PREPARATION TIME: 1 minute

seafood paella, spanish mama style

WHILE I WAS IN SPAIN as a teenager living with my Spanish 'mama' Julia and her family, we used to go to their farm on weekends in the heart of Castilla-La Mancha. Julia gave me my first taste of paella – which doesn't resemble any 'paella' I've ever had outside Spain. She made hers over an open fire in an age-old iron paella pan. It was the best thing I had ever eaten. I asked her to teach me how she does it and have made it many times since. This stove-top version is the real deal.

1l	Fish Stock (page 40)
2	teaspoons sweet pimenton
	Coarse salt
4	tablespoons good Spanish extra virgin olive oil, plus more if needed
6	large prawns, heads and shells on
2	small lobsters, split in half lengthways (cut through the eyes first – the quickest, supposedly most humane way to kill a lobster)
1½	large onions, peeled and diced
1	red pepper, seeds and stem removed, cut into 2.5cm pieces
3	cloves garlic, peeled and finely chopped
400g	Bomba rice (I strongly recommend using Bomba rice if you can find it, but white risotto rice will work just fine too.)
1	dozen small clams, scrubbed (See Salt Scrubs for Clams, page 43)
2	fillets flat white fish (such as sole), cut into 5cm-wide pieces
2	tablespoons roughly chopped fresh parsley
2	lemons, cut into wedges, for serving

Combine the fish stock, pimenton and salt to taste in a large saucepan and keep warm over a low heat. Meanwhile, heat the olive oil until nearly smoking in a 40cm paella pan set on a barbecue or paella burner, or straddling 2 burners. Add the prawns and cook, flipping occasionally, for 6–7 minutes, or until a bit browned. Remove to a plate and then add the lobsters to the pan shell side down and cook for 4½ minutes, flip, and cook for another 4½ minutes. Put the lobsters on the plate with the prawns. If the pan is a bit dry, add a few more tablespoons of olive oil. Turn the heat down to medium, add the onions, pepper and garlic and cook, stirring, for about 10 minutes, or until just softened. Pour the rice in the pan in an even cross (this is the way I was taught and I don't mess with tradition) and then stir to combine with the vegetables. Add the stock, bring to the boil and then lower the heat to a simmer and cook for 10 minutes. Arrange the prawns, lobsters, clams and fish on top of the rice, cover with a large piece of foil, and cook for 10 minutes. Remove the foil and cook for 5 more minutes. The clams should be open and the rice should be cooked through. You might start to hear a crackling sound – this is a good thing, it means you're forming a crust at the bottom of the pan (the *soccarat*), which distinguishes all great paellas. Remove the pan from the heat source, cover with your large piece of foil, and let it sit undisturbed for 15 minutes before serving, sprinkled with parsley.

Bring the pan to the table, scoop plenty of everything onto everyone's plates and encourage your guests to squeeze lots of lemon on their dinner.

 SERVES: 1 if you're me, but actually 4–6
ACTIVE PREPARATION TIME: 40 minutes
TOTAL PREPARATION TIME: a little over 1 hour

vegetable paella

WHEN I HAVE VEGETARIAN OR VEGAN friends coming for a festive meal and I imagine they are tired of being served pasta with tomato sauce at a dinner party, I like to mix things up with paella. You can improvise this recipe by adding other vegetables, but make sure you taste the broth along the way to ensure it has a lot of flavour and is well seasoned.

1l	Vegetable Stock (page 36)
2	dried shiitake or porcini mushrooms
10	cloves garlic, 4 crushed and 6 finely chopped
	Large pinch saffron
½	teaspoon sweet pimenton
	Coarse salt
	Freshly ground black pepper
1	large aubergine cut into 8mm-thick slices, ends discarded
125ml	olive oil
1	onion, finely diced
1	large tomato
2	red peppers, seeds and stem removed, cut into 2.5cm pieces
400g	Bomba rice (I strongly recommend using Bomba rice if you can find it, but white risotto rice will work just fine too.)
8	small artichokes, trimmed and steamed for 20 minutes, cut in half and chokes discarded
150g	frozen peas
3	lemons, 2 cut into wedges
	Quick Pimenton Aioli (page 173)

Combine the stock with the mushrooms and the 4 cloves of crushed garlic in a large saucepan and boil over high heat for 10 minutes. Lower the heat, add the saffron and pimenton and simmer for an additional 10 minutes to thoroughly combine the flavours. The secret to this recipe is a well-seasoned broth, so season to taste with salt and pepper and more saffron and/or pimenton if necessary. Keep warm over a low heat.

Meanwhile, prepare the aubergine. Sprinkle both sides of the aubergine slices with a bit of salt and lay them between sheets of kitchen paper for at least 15 minutes. Cut the aubergine into 2.5cm pieces. Heat half the olive oil in a large sauté pan set over medium heat and cook 2 cloves of the chopped garlic until fragrant, about a minute. Add the pieces of aubergine to the pan and cook for 12–15 minutes, stirring now and then, until browned and softened. Set aside.

Meanwhile, heat the remaining olive oil in a 40–45cm paella pan over high heat until just beginning to smoke. Turn the heat down to medium, add the onion and the 4 remaining cloves of chopped garlic, and cook, stirring, until just beginning to soften, about 5 minutes. Coarsely grate in the tomato, discarding the skin. Stir together and cook for another 2 minutes. Add the peppers and continue to cook the vegetables together until softened, another 10 minutes. Stir in the cooked aubergine. At this point the vegetable mixture can be set aside for up to 2 hours or refrigerated overnight.

When you're ready to roll, place the paella pan with the vegetables over high heat and pour the rice into the pan in an even cross (this is how I was taught). Add the stock and stir to combine everything. Bring to the boil and then lower the heat to a simmer. Arrange the artichokes and peas on top and simmer until the rice is cooked through, about 35 minutes. Remove the pan from the heat source, cover with a large piece of foil and let it sit undisturbed for 15 minutes. Alternatively you can cook the paella outside over a not-too-hot barbecue. Squeeze the juice of the lemon over the paella. Serve with lemon wedges and the Quick Pimenton Aioli, which is great for artichoke dipping.

SERVES: 6 • ACTIVE PREPARATION TIME: 1 hour • TOTAL PREPARATION TIME: 1½ hours

quick pimenton aioli

125ml	Vegenaise (or your favourite mayonnaise)	½ teaspoon fresh lemon juice
1	small clove garlic, finely chopped or grated	Coarse salt
¼	teaspoon pimenton	Freshly ground black pepper

Whisk everything together, adding more of any ingredient to suit your taste.

   YIELD: 125ml • ACTIVE & TOTAL PREPARATION TIME: 10 minutes

wood oven pizzas

WE'VE GOT A WOOD-BURNING pizza oven in the garden – a luxury, I know, but it's one of the best investments I've ever made. Home-made pizza is not only incredibly delicious, but it is an opportunity for a real family activity – and it's fun! My kids love to assemble their own versions – my daughter likes sauce and olives, my son likes a classic margarita. I love four-cheese (mozzarella, Parmesan, Gorgonzola and fontina with a splash of truffle oil) or a pissaladière (slowly cooked onions, garlic, anchovies and black olives). As long as you're making home-made dough, you can't go wrong. And this works really well in a conventional oven with a pizza stone – just set your oven as high as it will go and let the stone get all the way up to temperature before you put your first pizza in.

for the dough

550ml	warm water
2	tablespoons granulated sugar
3	sachets or 20g dried yeast
	About 600g strong bread flour, plus more for kneading and dusting
1½	tablespoons extra virgin olive oil
1	tablespoon coarse salt

for the sauce

2	tablespoons extra virgin olive oil
4	cloves garlic, peeled and left whole
2	400g cans whole peeled tomatoes with their juice
1	teaspoon coarse salt

for the toppings (choose a couple, or as many as you like)

Fresh mozzarella

Fresh basil leaves

Your best, highest-quality olive oil

Slowly cooked onions (For 2 pizzas, I like to cut 3 onions into thin rounds and cook them on medium heat with a few spoonfuls of olive oil, a bay leaf and a sprig of thyme until they're very soft and totally collapsed and caramelized, a good 25 minutes.)

Olive oil-packed Spanish anchovies

Olives

Parmesan cheese

Gorgonzola cheese

Truffle oil

If you have a wood fire, get it going a couple of hours before you want to eat pizza. If not, preheat a pizza stone in your oven at the highest heat it can go to for at least 1 hour before eating.

For the dough, whisk together 175ml water, the sugar and the yeast in a large bowl and let stand until surface has a few little bubbles and is creamy, about 5 minutes. Add 375ml water, 425g flour, olive oil and salt, and stir until smooth. While stirring, gradually add up to another 125g flour until the dough starts to pull itself from the edges of the bowl.

Knead the dough on a generously floured surface until elastic and smooth – it will take about 8 minutes of hard work. Dust the surface with flour as you go – you don't want the dough to stick. Form the kneaded dough into a ball, dust with flour and gently place in a large bowl and cover with clingfilm. Let it rise in a warm spot until doubled, about 1½ hours. (You can let it sit for up to a couple of hours or even overnight in the refrigerator.)

For the sauce, meanwhile, heat the olive oil in a medium saucepan over medium heat with the garlic. Add the tomatoes and their juice and salt and bring to the boil. Lower the heat and let the sauce simmer for 1 hour. Cool it to room temperature and purée in a blender.

To assemble the pizzas, break off pieces of the dough and stretch them with your fingers until quite thin. Flour your pizza peel (the board you slide under the pizza) and place the dough on top (better to do this first as opposed to trying to transfer your fully loaded pizza onto the peel).

For the toppings, dress each pizza however you'd like. A slick of tomato sauce, a few torn pieces of mozzarella and basil and a drizzle of olive oil is classic for a reason. I like a heap of slowly cooked onions, a few anchovies and some black olives. Four-cheese is also a winner, and, anointed with a little truffle oil, is a slice of heaven. However you choose, be sure to drizzle each pizza with good olive oil before sliding it into your hot oven. If you get them really thin and your oven is super hot, each pizza will cook in about 2 minutes. Most regular ovens will take more like 6 minutes. You're looking for a slightly charred crust and a top that is bubbling.

YIELD: 4–6 15cm pizzas · ACTIVE PREPARATION TIME: 1 hour
TOTAL PREPARATION TIME: about 2½ hours

ten-hour chicken

THIS DISH IS GREAT when you are going to work in the morning but want a no-fuss meal when you get home. The long, slow cooking means the chicken basically braises in its own juices all day long. What you get is a falling-off-the-bone chicken, very tender and very juicy. Just make sure that the breast is down and you make a nice airtight seal with the foil. Then when you get home, remove the foil, turn the chicken over and crisp up the skin, and you have one of the easiest working-parent dinners ever.

1 organic whole chicken (1.4–1.8kg), washed and dried (See Salt Scrubs for Poultry, page 43)

1 lemon, halved

Coarse salt

Freshly ground black pepper

½ bunch fresh thyme

Half a head of garlic, peeled

Preheat the oven to 110°C (200°F) gas ¼.

Place the chicken in a rectangular roasting tin breast side down. Squeeze the lemon halves over the chicken in the tin. Generously sprinkle the chicken with salt and pepper all over (front and back, inside and out). Tuck the thyme and the lemon halves and 3–4 cloves of garlic in the cavity. Place the remaining garlic cloves around the tin. Wrap the roasting tin tightly with foil and put it in the oven for, no joke, 9½ hours.

Take the chicken out of the oven and boost the heat to 200°C (400°F) gas 6, on fan heat if possible. Unwrap the dish, flip the chicken so it's lying on its back, breast side up, and sprinkle with more salt and pepper. Roast for 15–20 minutes, or until it's nicely browned. Let the chicken cool slightly, then carve and serve with all of its lovely juices.

SERVES: 4 · ACTIVE PREPARATION TIME: 10 minutes · TOTAL PREPARATION TIME: about 10 hours
You put it on in the morning and don't worry about it until the evening.

grilled salmon with home-made teriyaki sauce

THIS DELICIOUS SALMON TERIYAKI RECIPE is the way that I got my son eating salmon (full of protein, omegas, etc., salmon has been hailed as a miracle food). The sauce has honey in it, so it gets crispy and sweet as it caramelizes. I like to make bigger fillets for the older set and bite-sized ones for the kids. It is really good.

- 4 tablespoons soy sauce
- 2 tablespoons mirin
- 3 tablespoons honey
- 5 tablespoons water
- 1 teaspoon peeled and finely grated ginger
- 2 sprigs fresh coriander
- 4 175g salmon fillets, skin discarded
- 1 tablespoon finely chopped fresh chives, for serving

Combine the soy sauce, mirin, honey, water, ginger and coriander in a small saucepan over high heat. Once it boils, turn the heat to low and let it simmer for 2 minutes. Remove the saucepan from the heat and let the sauce cool down. Once it's cool, pour into a large bowl or plastic bag and add the salmon. Marinate in the fridge for at least an hour, up to overnight.

When you're ready to eat, preheat the grill.

Put the salmon on a heavy baking sheet with whatever sauce adheres to it and grill until cooked to your liking, 7–8 minutes. While it's cooking, strain the extra sauce into a clean saucepan, bring to the boil, and let it reduce.

To serve, drizzle the cooked salmon with some of the extra sauce and a sprinkle of chives.

make it kid friendly   Cut some of the salmon into 2.5cm cubes, grill alongside the larger pieces and serve without the chives – kids love these, especially if you call the teriyaki 'honey sauce'.

make it vegan   Replace the salmon with tofu.

SERVES: 4 · ACTIVE PREPARATION TIME: 20 minutes
TOTAL PREPARATION TIME: 1½ hours up to overnight

perfect roast chinese duck

THIS IS DEFINITELY FOR A PARTY meal or a big Sunday dinner. It takes some effort, but it's worth it. You must make the duck broth for the Duck Broth with Soba (page 52) the next day! Serve with Sesame Pancakes – or ready-made Chinese pancakes or flour tortillas – Red Miso Hoisin, cucumber matchsticks and sliced spring onions.

1 organic large duck, washed and dried (See Salt Scrubs for Poultry, page 43)

Coarse salt

Freshly ground black pepper

1 small onion, peeled and quartered

2 star anise

⅛ teaspoon ground cloves

50g dark brown sugar (unrefined if possible)

Boiling water

1 cucumber, cut into matchsticks, for serving

1 bunch spring onions, shredded, for serving

Sesame Pancakes (page 180), for serving

Red Miso Hoisin (page 180), for serving

Preheat the oven to 180°C (350°F) gas 4.

Trim off excess skin from the opening to the cavity and from the back end of the duck (render it and save it for frying potatoes if you like). Use your fingers and the tip of a paring knife to slip underneath the skin covering the breast, loosening it and being careful not to tear it. Pierce the skin all over with the paring knife (approximately 50 times), but do not pierce the meat itself. This is to ensure that all the fat renders during cooking and you'll be rewarded with delicious, crispy skin.

Put the duck in a large roasting tin. Generously sprinkle salt and pepper over it, top to bottom, front and back. Stuff the cavity with the onion and star anise. Put the duck breast side up in the pan and sprinkle with ground cloves. Sprinkle the brown sugar all round the duck, not on it. Pour enough boiling water over the duck and into the tin to come up 2.5cm (to tighten the skin).

Cover the tin very tightly with foil. Bake for 1 hour, flip it, cover it again with the foil, and bake for an additional hour. Transfer the duck to a plate and let it cool.

Meanwhile, put the roasting tin on the hob and boil the liquid over high heat for 20–30 minutes, or until reduced by about half. Cool slightly and pour it into a storage container. Wrap up both the duck and the liquid and refrigerate overnight.

To finish the duck, preheat the oven to 260°C (500°F) highest setting gas.

Roast the duck for 25 minutes, or until crispy and browned. Let it rest for at least 10 minutes before serving.

To serve, use your reserved pan juices. A significant amount of fat should be hardened on the top – scoop it off and discard. Put the dark brown juice in a small saucepan and warm it over medium heat. Carve the duck into thin slices. Pour the warm juice over the slices. Wrap up bits of duck, cucumbers and spring onions in Sesame Pancakes spread with Red Miso Hoisin sauce.

SERVES: 4 • **ACTIVE PREPARATION TIME:** 20 minutes
TOTAL PREPARATION TIME: 2½ hours plus overnight refrigeration

sesame pancakes

125g unbleached plain flour

375ml rice milk

Pinch salt

2 teaspoons toasted sesame oil

1 teaspoon vegetable oil

Whisk together the flour, milk, salt and sesame oil. Heat a small non-stick frying pan (I use a 15cm frying pan) over medium heat. Pour in the vegetable oil and use kitchen paper to spread it evenly. Pour in 2 tablespoons of batter and swirl the pan to coat the bottom. Cook for about 30 seconds, or until browned on the bottom. Peel the pancake up from the pan and flip it (it's fastest to loosen the edges with a butter knife or rubber spatula and then lift it up with your fingers). Cook for about 30 seconds on the second side. The first one's usually a dud. That's OK. Continue the process until you run out of batter. You should end up with about a dozen pancakes.

note: You can make these ahead and then quickly heat them up for a few seconds on each side in a hot, non-stick pan – much easier than trying to make them all last minute!

 YIELD: about 1 dozen pancakes • ACTIVE & TOTAL PREPARATION TIME: 20 minutes

red miso hoisin

THIS IS SO MUCH HEALTHIER than a commercial version!

1 tablespoon grapeseed or vegetable oil

1 large clove garlic, peeled and finely chopped

½ teaspoon Chinese five-spice powder

125ml red miso

125ml real Vermont maple syrup

2 tablespoons brown rice vinegar

Heat the grapeseed oil in a small saucepan over medium heat. Add the garlic and five-spice powder and cook for about 30 seconds, or until wonderfully fragrant. Whisk in the remaining ingredients, bring to the boil, and cook, whisking or stirring constantly, for 3–4 minutes, or until slightly thickened. Let the sauce cool before using. It keeps well in the refrigerator for a few days.

 YIELD: about 250ml • ACTIVE & TOTAL PREPARATION TIME: about 5 minutes

crab boil

SO MY DECEASED MATERNAL GRANDMOTHER, Mutti, was a great entertainer (but not actually that nice one on one, at least to me!). She was amazing at a party and she used to throw them all the time. She was famous for them. One of her old-school recipes was this crab boil for a dinner party. Her original method for making the crab is just as I have it here. It works beautifully. I modified the sauce a bit as the original used a lot of pre-made sauces with too many preservatives.

1	fresh bay leaf
5	black peppercorns
2	cloves
	Pinch coarse salt
1	large clove garlic, peeled and crushed
1	lemon, halved
2	large live crabs
	Sauce for Crab Boil (recipe follows)

Fill your largest saucepan with water, add the bay leaf, peppercorns, cloves, salt and garlic, and squeeze in the juice from the lemon (throw the lemon halves into the pan too). Bring the seasoned water to the boil and let it boil for 10–15 minutes. Add the crabs and boil for 15 minutes. Remove them to a tray and let them sit until cool enough to handle. Get to work with a mallet and a pick, getting all the bits of meat out of the claws and body. You can do this for your guests and serve everyone a pile of pristine crabmeat with a bowl of sauce alongside or you can all stand in the kitchen and do it together, dipping bits of crab as you work.

 SERVES: 4 · ACTIVE PREPARATION TIME: 20 minutes · TOTAL PREPARATION TIME: 1 hour

 You can serve it cold.

sauce for crab boil

125ml	Vegenaise or mayo
1	generous tablespoon ketchup
2	teaspoons Dijon mustard
2	teaspoons prepared horseradish
2	teaspoons finely chopped fresh chives
4	cornichons, finely diced
	Coarse salt
	Freshly ground black pepper

Stir everything together, seasoning to taste with salt and pepper.

  YIELD: 175ml · ACTIVE & TOTAL PREPARATION TIME: 10 minutes

duck 'cassoulet'

I FIRST HAD DUCK CONFIT with my dad on a trip to Paris at a place called Josephine Chez Dumonet. I never realized how delicious, tender and yet crispy duck could be. When I discovered cassoulet (in which duck confit is the star) I was transported. When I stopped eating pork and red meat, I couldn't indulge in it any more, so I set out to make my own. This pork-free version is rich and deeply flavoured – a great one-pot weekend supper. I wish I could make it for my dad, he would go out of his mind.

2   410g cans cannellini beans, rinsed and drained

1   big dark green leaf from the outside of a leek

7   cloves garlic, peeled, 3 crushed, 4 finely sliced

    Coarse salt

    Bouquet garni of 3 sprigs fresh parsley, 1 sprig chervil, 2 cloves, 1 bay leaf, and 6 peppercorns

4   slices bacon (of whichever variety), fat removed from all but 1, chopped into lardons

1   medium onion, peeled and finely chopped

1   400g can whole peeled tomatoes with their juice

    Freshly ground black pepper

4   legs duck confit, excess fat scraped off (strain the fat and save it for cooking delicious potatoes!)

2   tablespoons extra virgin olive oil

½   day-old baguette, cut into coarse crumbs (or pulsed 10 times in a food processor)

1   tablespoon chopped fresh parsley

2   sprigs fresh thyme

Combine the beans, leek leaf, 1 clove of crushed garlic, a large pinch of salt and the bouquet garni in a large saucepan. Cover with cold water, bring to the boil and lower the heat. Let it simmer over low heat while you proceed.

In a large heavy casserole dish, cook the bacon over medium-high heat for 3 minutes, or until beginning to render and brown. Turn the heat to low and add the onion and the 4 cloves of sliced garlic. Cook for 15 minutes, keeping the heat low. Add the tomatoes and their juice, crushing them with a wooden spoon, a pinch of salt and a few healthy grinds of black pepper. Simmer on low for half an hour.

Meanwhile, put the duck legs in a large frying pan and set it over medium heat. Let the duck legs brown deeply on both sides, about 5 minutes a side, and remove to a plate, reserving the fat in the pan. Add the olive oil to the pan along with the 2 remaining cloves of crushed garlic, keeping the heat at medium. Add the breadcrumbs and cook, stirring, until fragrant, about 2 minutes. Remove from heat, discard the garlic and stir in the parsley.

At this point your tomato mixture should be cooked down. Drain the beans, reserving their cooking liquid and discarding the leek, garlic and bouquet garni. Stir the beans into the tomato mixture, nestle in the thyme and the duck legs. Season with salt and pepper.

At this point, you can wait up to a day or two to cook the cassoulet – refrigerate the bean and duck mixture, bean liquid and breadcrumbs separately and bring to room temperature before proceeding. Or, preheat the oven to 180°C (350°F) gas 4. To finish, scatter the breadcrumbs over the top of the cassoulet and evenly ladle over 375ml of the bean cooking liquid. Bake in the preheated oven until the breadcrumbs are nicely browned, about 30 minutes.

 SERVES: 4 · ACTIVE PREPARATION TIME: 1 hour · TOTAL PREPARATION TIME: 1½ hours

grilled 'baked stuffed' lobsters

BAKED, STUFFED LOBSTER HAS ALWAYS been one of my absolute favourite
East Coast special-occasion dinners. This version gets a smoky, charred flavour
from the barbecue, but is equally delish done under the grill. The trick of the
stuffing is to chop up the roe and liver (tomalley) and mix them in with the
other ingredients – also the Vegenaise adds a delicious moistness.

2 x 675g	lobsters
75g	fresh coarse breadcrumbs (pulse day-old bread in a food processor)
2½	tablespoons dry breadcrumbs
75g	unsalted butter, melted
75g	coarse crabmeat, shredded with your fingers
75g	prawns, chopped, or extra crabmeat
1	tablespoon finely chopped fresh parsley
½	teaspoon coarse salt
¼	teaspoon freshly ground black pepper
2	teaspoons fresh lemon juice
3	tablespoons Vegenaise or mayo

Preheat the barbecue to high.

Cut the lobsters in half: first insert a sharp knife swiftly through their
eyes and then cut straight down through their tails. Scoop out any roe and
finely chop it. In a large bowl, mix the roe with both the fresh and dried
breadcrumbs, 25g butter, the crab, prawns, parsley, salt, pepper, lemon juice
and 2 tablespoons of the Vegenaise. In a separate small bowl, whisk together
the remaining tablespoon of Vegenaise with the remaining butter. Evenly
divide the stuffing along the cut sides of the lobsters and evenly drizzle over
the Vegenaise-butter mixture. Carefully lay the lobsters on a large baking
tray and put the pan directly on the hot barbecue. Cover and cook for
15 minutes, or until the stuffing is browned (the barbecue acts as an oven)
and the lobster meat is just firm to the touch.

notes: You can make these indoors – simply roast them at 230°C (450°F)
gas 8 for about 15 minutes to cook everything through and then grill them for
2 minutes to brown the tops.

As an alternative to lobster, you can stuff the filling into butterflied tiger
prawns that you've seasoned with salt and pepper (these take only 10 minutes
to cook). Delish.

SERVES: 4 · ACTIVE PREPARATION TIME: 10 minutes · TOTAL PREPARATION TIME: ½ hour

You can stuff the lobsters ahead of time.

aunt evelyn's brisket (by way of grandma vicki & grandma dorothy)

MY FATHER'S BROTHER, BOBBY, married a girl named Evelyn a long, long time ago. Evelyn is a Sephardic Jew and had an amazing mother, the matriarch of the family, Grandma Vicki. My paternal grandmother, Dorothy, lived down the street from Grandma Vicki, and they would frequently break bread together. They all made brisket, and each family was famous for its own version. Although I have not eaten red meat for years, I remember the days of eating this brisket and loving the tender, falling-apart meat, which was always served with butter noodles. When I was working on the recipes for this family book, I felt I had to include a brisket to be true to the long line of Paltrow, Weigert, and Hertz women before me for whom this dish was so essential. We got all of the recipes together (one included dry-rubbing the meat with Lipton onion soup mix!) and devised a way to amalgamate and elevate all at the same time. Julia Turshen, my right hand in helping me put this book together, did the tasting with her mother and grandmother, and it got a big thumbs-up.

1.4kg	beef brisket joint
1	tablespoon paprika
2	cloves garlic, peeled and finely chopped
1	teaspoon coarse salt
½	teaspoon freshly ground black pepper
7	tablespoons extra virgin olive oil
2	large onions, peeled and thinly sliced
4	carrots, peeled and cut into 7.5cm pieces
500ml	good red wine
125ml	Chicken Stock (page 39)

Preheat the oven to 150°C (300°F) gas 2.

Trim the brisket of any excess fat. Meanwhile, stir together the paprika, garlic, salt, pepper and 1 tablespoon of the olive oil. Rub this spice mixture all over the brisket and let it sit at room temperature while you cook the vegetables.

Heat 2 tablespoons of the olive oil in a large sauté pan over medium-high heat. Cook the onions, stirring occasionally, until softened and lightly browned, about 10 minutes. Place the onions in the bottom of a 32 x 23cm casserole dish and return the pan to the heat with 2 additional tablespoons of olive oil. Add the carrots to the pan and cook, stirring occasionally, until lightly browned, about 5 minutes. Add the carrots to the onions. Return the pan to the hob, turn the heat to high and add 2 more tablespoons of olive oil. Deeply brown the brisket on both sides, about 4 minutes a side. Place the brisket on top of the vegetables. Add the wine to the pan, bring to the boil and let it cook for 3 minutes. Pour the wine and the chicken stock over the brisket and vegetables.

Cover the casserole tightly with foil and bake for 3 hours. Remove the brisket from the casserole and let it cool while you finish the sauce. Blend half of the cooked vegetables with about 250ml of the cooking liquid in a blender until smooth. Return the blended mixture to the remaining vegetables and juice (this helps to thicken the sauce). Slice the brisket as thinly as you like it and either serve immediately or place the slices in the sauce, wrap tightly and reheat in a 150°C (300°F) gas 2 oven when ready to serve.

SERVES: 4, with leftovers • ACTIVE PREPARATION TIME: 20 minutes • TOTAL PREPARATION TIME: 3–4 hours

side
dishes

A couple of great-looking little dishes can be so comforting and sometimes unexpected, all while celebrating or reinventing the vegetable it features. While rounding out a main dish with a perfect side really elevates the whole meal, sometimes my entire dinner will consist of lots of little veggie dishes, especially great for punching up the vegetarian excitement factor. In the summer when my favourite vegetarian friend, Stella McCartney, brings her family over, I like to double the recipes and make a vegetarian buffet, sometimes Italian (bruschetta, burrata with roasted beetroot, roasted peppers, stuffed artichokes, courgette flowers) or East Coast summer (garlic bread from GOOP.com, corn fritters and a simple bean salad).

sautéed greens with onions & soy sauce

THIS HEALTHY SIDE DISH has tons of flavour from the sharp greens, sweet onions and soy sauce. Winter greens have many nutrients, so I love for my family to partake of them.

2 tablespoons extra virgin olive oil

1 small onion, peeled and thinly sliced

450g seasonal greens (kale, Swiss chard, dandelion, etc.), stems removed and discarded, leaves washed and roughly torn

125ml water

1½ tablespoons soy sauce

Heat the olive oil in a large frying pan over medium-high heat. Cook the onion, stirring occasionally for 5–7 minutes, or until just softened and a little crisp on the edges. Add about half the greens and the water – these will wilt significantly after a minute or two. Add the remaining greens and stir for another 3 minutes, or until the greens are wilted but still maintain a little bite. Add the soy sauce, cook for one more minute and serve.

 SERVES: 4 generously · ACTIVE & TOTAL PREPARATION TIME: 10 minutes

roasted cauliflower

ROASTING CAULIFLOWER SLOWLY IN OLIVE OIL brings out incredible sweetness and crunch – two things that go over big with the little ones. My kids love these. They are great as a side or chopped into a vegetable salad.

1 head cauliflower, hard core discarded, cut into small florets

2 tablespoons extra virgin olive oil

Pinch coarse salt

Pinch freshly ground black pepper

Preheat the oven to 230°C (450°F) gas 8.

In a baking dish large enough to hold the cauliflower in one layer, toss all the ingredients together. Roast for 35 minutes, stirring occasionally, until the cauliflower is caramelized all over. So simple and so unbelievably good.

 SERVES: 4 • ACTIVE PREPARATION TIME: 5 minutes
TOTAL PREPARATION TIME: 40 minutes

crispy potato & garlic cake

I FIRST ATE SOMETHING AKIN to this dish at Chez L'Ami Louis in Paris, my father's favourite restaurant maybe in the world. They serve a sizzling hot, garlicky version of this pie – which I started re-creating in my own kitchen a few years ago. I'm not sure how they do theirs, but this is definitely an homage to their masterpiece. I love it served with a roast or duck confit, French style.

2 large baking potatoes (each about 300g), peeled

5 tablespoons duck fat (1 tablespoon is for the pan, or you can use butter)

4 tablespoons extra virgin olive oil

3 cloves garlic, peeled, 2 crushed, 1 very finely chopped

Coarse salt

1 tablespoon finely chopped fresh parsley

Preheat the grill.

Boil the potatoes for 20 minutes and let them cool before slicing them into 3mm-thick slices. Heat a spoonful each of the duck fat and the olive oil in a large non-stick frying pan over medium heat. Add 1 of the crushed garlic cloves and as many potato slices as can fit in one layer. Cook for about 3 minutes a side, or until lightly browned. Remove to a kitchen-paper–lined plate and repeat with the remaining fat and potatoes, replacing the garlic cloves when they get too brown.

Coat a small (15–20cm) cast-iron frying pan with the last tablespoon of duck fat. Line the bottom with a single layer of potato slices, sprinkle with salt and add another layer. Repeat this process, pressing each layer down hard with the back of a wooden spoon and lightly salting as you go until you've layered all your potatoes. Pressing them down is what will keep the cake together, so don't be too gentle. Stick the cake under the grill until really browned and crispy, about 5 minutes. Invert it onto a plate and scatter with the 1 clove of finely chopped garlic, parsley and bit more salt if you like. Cut into wedges and serve.

SERVES: 4 • ACTIVE & TOTAL PREPARATION TIME: a little under 1 hour

This can be made ahead up until the point of grilling.

maple-dijon roasted winter vegetables

KIDS AND ADULTS ALIKE DEVOUR these sweet roasted vegetables. Any hearty root vegetables will work – butternut squash, turnips, etc. Whatever the combo, the maple syrup and mustard marry the flavours and turn them into a crowd pleaser.

3 tablespoons real Vermont maple syrup

3 tablespoons Dijon mustard

3 tablespoons extra virgin olive oil

½ teaspoon coarse salt

½ teaspoon freshly ground black pepper

1 large sweet potato, peeled and cut into 7.5cm sticks about 1cm thick (like French fries)

4 parsnips, peeled and cut into 7.5cm sticks about 1cm thick (like French fries)

4 carrots, peeled and cut into 7.5cm sticks about 1cm thick (like French fries)

Preheat the oven to 220°C (425°F) gas 7.

Mix together the maple syrup, mustard, olive oil, salt and pepper. Toss together with the vegetables on a baking sheet. Roast, stirring occasionally, until browned and cooked through, about 25 minutes.

 **SERVES:** 4 • **ACTIVE PREPARATION TIME:** 10 minutes
TOTAL PREPARATION TIME: about ½ hour

caramelized
brussels sprouts

I HAVE CONVERTED MANY a sprout cynic with these crispy, crunchy Brussels sprouts. I must make these three times a week when they are in season. They go with anything and are the opposite of your grandmother's overboiled cabbage-tasting variety.

450g Brussels sprouts, trimmed

2 tablespoons extra virgin olive oil

A few generous pinches coarse salt

Your best, highest-quality olive oil, for serving

½ lemon, for serving

Steam the Brussels sprouts for 7 minutes, or until just tender. Let them cool a bit and then cut each in half lengthways.

Heat the olive oil in a large frying pan over medium-high heat. Place the Brussels sprouts in a single layer cut side down (in batches if necessary). Leave them for 4–5 minutes, allowing them to brown thoroughly and evenly – don't give in to the temptation to stir and toss them! Keep an eye on them though – the key is to have the heat high enough to brown them but low enough not to burn them. When they've browned, flip each one and let the other side colour, an additional 3 minutes or so. Remove to a serving dish, sprinkle with the salt, drizzle with your best olive oil and squeeze the lemon over the Brussel sprouts, trying to get a bit of juice on each one. Delish.

SERVES: 4 • ACTIVE & TOTAL PREPARATION TIME: 20 minutes

fried rice with kale & spring onions

MY KIDS CALL THIS GREEN RICE and they love it. Oh how my heart leaps when I see them munching down kale with brown rice. The smaller you cut the kale, the more it becomes about the rice. I love it when something this nutritious tastes so good.

225g kale, stems discarded

1½ tablespoons vegetable oil

2 cloves garlic, peeled and very finely chopped

3 large spring onions, cut into 3mm diagonal slices

175g brown rice, cooked

1½ tablespoons soy sauce

Cut the kale leaves in half lengthways and then cut crossways into very thin ribbons (chiffonade). Steam the kale for 7 minutes.

Meanwhile, heat the vegetable oil in a large saucepan over medium-low heat. Add the garlic and cook, stirring, for 2 minutes, being careful not to brown the garlic. Raise the heat to medium and add the steamed kale and spring onions. Cook for 2 minutes and then add the rice and cook for another 2 minutes, stirring. Add the soy sauce and cook for 30 seconds more.

 SERVES: 4 · ACTIVE & TOTAL PREPARATION TIME: 15 minutes

roasted sweet potatoes with spices

SWEET POTATOES ARE A BIG family fave. These accentuate the innate sweetness with some maple syrup – making them soft and caramelized. The spices make them nice for the holidays as well.

550g	sweet potatoes (about 2 medium), peeled
5	tablespoons real Vermont maple syrup
2	tablespoons vegetable oil
¼	teaspoon ground cinnamon
⅛	teaspoon ground cloves
1	large orange
1	star anise

Preheat the oven to 190°C (375°F) gas 5.

Cut each sweet potato in half horizontally and then cut each half into 8mm-thick slices (about 4 slices per half depending on the size of the sweet potato). Lay the sweet potatoes in a single layer in a large earthenware baking dish that's been lined with a piece of baking paper (makes washing up much easier).

Mix the maple syrup, vegetable oil, cinnamon and cloves together in a small bowl. Peel off 2 large strips of rind from the orange. Cut the orange in half and squeeze the juice from one half into the bowl with the maple syrup mixture. Pour this mixture evenly over the sweet potatoes, nestle in the strips of rind, and the star anise. Bake for 45 minutes, or until the sweet potatoes are soft.

SERVES: 4 · ACTIVE PREPARATION TIME: 10 minutes
TOTAL PREPARATION TIME: a little less than 1 hour

kale crisps

THESE THINGS ARE A SUREFIRE WAY to get your family eating this
nutrient-rich vegetable. They crisp up in the oven and sort of mimic potato
crisps. My kids eat them like they actually are potato crisps: they don't stop.

1 big bunch kale, stems
discarded and leaves torn
into roughly 3.5cm pieces

2 tablespoons extra virgin
olive oil

Coarse salt

Preheat the oven to 200°C (400°F) gas 6.

Toss the kale with the olive oil and spread out on two baking sheets.
Sprinkle with coarse salt and roast for 12–15 minutes, or until lightly browned
and crispy. Eat like potato crisps.

SERVES: 4 • ACTIVE PREPARATION TIME: 2 minutes • TOTAL PREPARATION TIME: 15 minutes

deli coleslaw

I HAVE YET TO FIND deli coleslaw that's the real deal in England (where I
live during the school year). This one really hits the spot when I'm dreaming
of a New York deli lunch or a BBQ. It's got that authentic taste. I put it directly
on my sandwiches.

½ small green cabbage,
coarsely grated

Coarse salt

½ carrot, peeled and
coarsely grated

125ml Vegenaise or mayo

2 teaspoons cider vinegar

2 teaspoons granulated
sugar

Toss the cabbage with a healthy pinch of salt and let sit for at least
10 minutes. Add the rest of the ingredients and stir to combine. Let the
coleslaw get to know itself for at least an hour or 2, but this is really best
when you let it sit overnight.

SERVES: 4 • ACTIVE PREPARATION TIME: 15 minutes
TOTAL PREPARATION TIME: 15 minutes plus at least 1 hour resting

french fries: two ways

HERE WE HAVE TWO VERSIONS of one of my favourite foods on earth: the French fry. The 'no-fry' version produces a crispy, delicious chip when you don't want the deep-fry effect on your health. The fried version is, well, fried, and therefore even more delicious.

NO-FRY FRIES

2 large King Edward potatoes (each about 300g), peeled

2 tablespoons olive oil

¾ teaspoon coarse salt

Preheat the oven to 230°C (450°F) gas 8.

Cut each potato in half horizontally and then cut each half into long, 8mm-thick sticks. Put the potatoes in a bowl of cold water as you're cutting them. Dry them completely on kitchen paper (dry potatoes = crispy French fries). Coat the potatoes with the olive oil and sprinkle with the salt. Roast on a wire rack set on top of a baking sheet until browned and cooked through, turning a few times as you go, about 25 minutes.

 SERVES: 4 • ACTIVE PREPARATION TIME: 10 minutes • TOTAL PREPARATION TIME: ½ hour

REAL FRENCH FRIES

2 large dense floury (not waxy) baking potatoes (each about 300g), peeled

Safflower oil for frying

Coarse salt

Cut each potato in half horizontally and then cut each half into long, 8mm-thick sticks. Put the potatoes in a bowl of cold water as you're cutting them and let them soak for at least ½ hour and up to overnight. Dry them completely on clean tea towels, really paying attention to each side (painstaking, yes, but worth it, as dry potatoes = crispy French fries). In a deep-fat fryer or large heavy saucepan, heat enough safflower oil for deep-frying (the oil should be at least 18cm deep) to 148°C (300°F). Fry the potatoes in batches for 4–5 minutes, stirring a bit with a slotted spoon, until light golden brown. Drain the potatoes on a wire rack set on top of a baking tray and let them cool as you continue with the remaining potatoes. Once all the potatoes have been through the first fry, raise the heat to 190°C (375°F) and fry them again in batches for about 2 more minutes or until darker brown and crisp. Drain them on a rack, sprinkle liberally with salt and serve immediately.

 SERVES: 4 • ACTIVE PREPARATION TIME: 30 minutes • TOTAL PREPARATION TIME: 1 hour

polenta with fresh corn

POLENTA IS A WONDERFUL CREAMY GRAIN, very healthy, and a neutral flavour – making it a canvas to showcase your favourite ingredients like cheeses, truffles, veggies and the like. During the summer when sweetcorn is rife, I like to stir it into polenta for a double hit of corn – a corn celebration. You can cut the leftovers into squares and fry them topped with Parmesan.

1l	water
170g	non-instant polenta
	Coarse salt
	Kernels from 1 fresh corn cob
125ml	milk
4	tablespoons cream
	Freshly ground black pepper
1	tablespoon roughly chopped fresh chives, for serving

Bring the water to the boil in a medium saucepan. Slowly whisk in the polenta and a pinch of salt. Turn the heat as low as it can go, put a lid on slightly ajar and cook the polenta for 40 minutes, stirring every 5–10 minutes. Add the corn, milk and cream and cook for 5 minutes. Season with salt and pepper and serve sprinkled with chives.

 SERVES: 4 • ACTIVE PREPARATION TIME: 20 minutes • TOTAL PREPARATION TIME: 50 minutes

stuffed artichokes with bread & tomatoes

I WANTED TO RE-CREATE one of my favourite side dishes I enjoyed at DaSilvano's, stuffed artichokes. After a few tries, I came up with this recipe. It takes a typical northern Italian pairing – day-old bread and tomatoes – and puts it in a steamed artichoke. It's a lovely side, especially with extra vinaigrette in which to dip the artichoke leaves – or it can serve as a light lunch.

4	artichokes, top 2cm and tough outer leaves cut off and discarded
150ml	extra virgin olive oil
3	tablespoons red wine vinegar
	Coarse salt
	Freshly ground black pepper
200g	day-old 1cm bread cubes (about ½ stale baguette will do)
450g	cherry tomatoes, quartered
	Handful fresh basil leaves, torn
1	lemon

Steam the artichokes for 45 minutes.

Meanwhile, whisk together 125ml olive oil and the vinegar and season with salt and pepper. Fold in the bread cubes. If they're really dry, add a spoonful of warm water. Using your hands, crush in the tomatoes and stir in the basil. Let the bread mixture sit while the artichokes are cooking.

When the artichokes are cooked through, let them sit for 10 or 15 minutes to cool. Using a soup spoon, scoop out the thistly chokes. Squeeze the lemon over the cavity of each artichoke and stuff with the bread salad. Drizzle over the remaining olive oil. Serve at room temperature.

 SERVES: 4 · ACTIVE PREPARATION TIME: 10 minutes · TOTAL PREPARATION TIME: 1 hour

bruce's dip

MY DAD USED TO WHIP UP this dip and serve it in half of a ripe
avocado – it was a summertime staple with a sandwich on the side.

250ml Vegenaise or mayo	Mix it all up.
125ml sour cream	
2 tablespoons finely chopped fresh parsley	
½ teaspoon Dijon mustard	
2 spring onions, finely sliced	
1 clove garlic, peeled and finely chopped or pushed through a press	
½ teaspoon fresh lemon juice	
A few grinds black pepper	
Pinch coarse salt	
1½ tablespoons capers, finely chopped	
¼ teaspoon celery seeds	

 SERVES: 4 • **ACTIVE & TOTAL PREPARATION TIME: 5 minutes**

corn fritters

MY GREAT FRIEND ROB (the husband of my oldest and best friend, Mary)
made a version of these a few summers ago. I loved them so much I decided
to try my own. These are wonderful when the summer corn is sweet and
abundant – I like them as a side dish or served on a bed of rocket as a main
course for lunch.

4	fresh corn cobs, husks removed
1	organic large egg, beaten
35g	Parmesan cheese, grated
25g	mature Cheddar cheese, grated
2	spring onions (white and light green parts), finely sliced
25g	unbleached plain flour
1½	teaspoons cornflour
¼	teaspoon freshly ground black pepper
¼	teaspoon coarse salt, plus more for finishing
4	tablespoons vegetable oil
10	fresh large basil leaves
2	tablespoons fresh coriander leaves

Cut the corn kernels off the cobs and discard the cobs. Combine the corn,
egg, cheeses, spring onions, flour, cornflour, pepper and ¼ teaspoon of salt
together in a large mixing bowl. Heat the vegetable oil in a medium non-stick
frying pan over medium-high heat. Pour about 4 tablespoons of the fritter
batter into the pan and fry for 2 minutes on each side, or until dark golden
brown and very attractive. Drain the fritters on kitchen paper, sprinkle with
salt and keep warm while you repeat the process with the remaining batter.
Roughly chop the basil and coriander leaves and scatter on top of the fritters.

 YIELD: 8 fritters • ACTIVE & TOTAL PREPARATION TIME: 20 minutes

courgette flowers with anchovies & mozzarella

WHEN I PASS A FLOWERING COURGETTE plant in a garden, my heart skips a beat. They are so delicious stuffed and fried, it's crazy. I have friends who make them with meat in the centre but my favourite is this version – with anchovies and mozzarella. You can substitute a squeeze of lemon with its zest for anchovies to make a vegetarian version.

75g	unbleached plain flour
1½	tablespoons extra virgin olive oil
175ml	sparkling water or soda water
	Coarse salt
175g	fresh mozzarella (water packed), coarsely grated
6	anchovy fillets, finely chopped
¼	teaspoon freshly ground black pepper
20	small courgette flowers
	Safflower or groundnut oil, for frying
1	lemon, halved, for serving

Whisk the flour together with the olive oil in a large bowl – the mixture will be lumpy. Whisk the fizzy water into the mixture until the batter is smooth. Season with a large pinch of salt, cover with clingfilm, and let sit for at least 30 minutes.

Meanwhile, mix together the mozzarella, anchovies, pepper and a pinch of salt in a mixing bowl with a wooden spoon. Carefully open each courgette flower and stuff it with a generous tablespoon of filling, twisting the top ever so gently just to keep everything inside – you want to try not to tear the flowers, but a break or two is inevitable, so don't drive yourself crazy. At this point, the batter and the flowers can be set aside for up to a couple of hours.

When you're ready to eat, heat up 2.5cm of oil in a large cast-iron frying pan or other heavy pan with a bit of height over medium-high heat. When a drop of water or small cube of bread sizzles on contact, dip each courgette flower into the batter just to coat it and carefully slip it into the oil. Fill the pan with as many flowers as will fit in a single layer without overcrowding. Brown the flowers on both sides (about 45 seconds a side) and then drain on kitchen paper. Serve hot, squeezing a bit of lemon juice and sprinkling salt over each.

SERVES: 4 · ACTIVE & TOTAL PREPARATION TIME: 45 minutes

You can make this ahead up to the point of frying.

bruschetta (or 'garlic toast' as my daughter calls it)

THIS IS ONE OF MY most asked-for sides, and probably the easiest. A slightly charred, garlic-and-oil-rubbed bread that makes any meal sing. The better and fresher the bread, the better the bruschetta, so it's definitely worth visiting the bakery for a rustic loaf such as pane Pugliese to maximize the perfection.

1 loaf pane Pugliese (or your favourite rustic bread), cut into 2cm-thick slices

2 large cloves garlic, peeled and cut in half

Extra virgin olive oil

Coarse salt

Grill the bread under a medium heat for about a minute on each side, or until toasted and just barely charred at spots. Rub both sides of bread with the cut sides of garlic. Drizzle one side generously with olive oil (at least 1½ tablespoons per slice). Sprinkle with coarse salt and serve.

SERVES: 4 • ACTIVE & TOTAL PREPARATION TIME: 10 minutes

fragrant jasmine rice

JASMINE RICE IS A LIFESAVER — it cooks so quickly, it's perfect for a last-minute grain. This version uses star anise and cardamom to accent the fine grain with some Asian flavour.

200g	jasmine rice (or substitute brown jasmine rice for a healthy alternative and follow timing directions)
425ml	water
1	whole star anise
2	whole cardamom pods, seeds separated and pods discarded
	Big pinch Maldon salt

Combine everything in a saucepan, bring to the boil, lower to a simmer, cover and cook for 15 minutes. Turn off the heat and let the rice sit for 10 minutes with the lid on. Fluff with a fork and serve.

note: Follow the rice-to-water ratio on whatever brand of rice you use.

SERVES: 4 • ACTIVE PREPARATION TIME: 5 minutes
TOTAL PREPARATION TIME: 25 minutes

breakfast

They say that breakfast is the most important meal of the day. . . I have some real breakfast fanatics in my house who would agree with that sentiment. With barely any extra effort, breakfast is an opportunity to speak to your loved ones' individualism. Pancakes plain? With chocolate chips and bananas? Thinned out to make a crepe with Nutella or Gruyère? Everyone can express their tastes, quirky or not. Bagel toasted with smoked salmon and cream cheese? Buttered? Untoasted onion bagel with peanut butter and jam? – not OK by the way. Food preferences are easy to contend with – set out a large bowl of granola and have all different fixin's on the side – berries, flax meal, yogurt, cow's milk, soya milk, hemp milk. Choices abound with only minor adjustments for the cook . . . making everyone feel loved, with their breakfast served just the way they like it.

artichoke & parmesan frittata

I MAKE FRITTATAS FREQUENTLY when people come over for brunch. They are easy and delicious and you can use whatever is in the fridge – or in season. You really can follow the technique below and dream up anything you like. They can be served anywhere from hot to room temperature, a plus for reducing stress when serving multiple dishes at brunch.

15g	unsalted butter
1	tablespoon extra virgin olive oil
2	large shallots, peeled and thinly sliced
175g	cooked artichoke hearts, cut into 5mm-thick slices
1	teaspoon fresh tarragon leaves, thinly sliced
	Coarse salt
	Freshly ground black pepper
6	organic large eggs
125ml	milk
50g	Parmesan cheese, grated

Preheat the oven to 190°C (375°F) gas 5.

Heat the butter and olive oil over medium heat in a 25cm cast-iron frying pan. Sauté the shallots until soft and just barely browned, about 6 minutes. Add the artichokes and tarragon and season with salt and pepper to taste.

Meanwhile, beat the eggs and milk to combine in a mixing bowl. Pour over the shallots and artichokes. Let it cook for about 5 minutes, or until just set on the edges (it will still be very runny in the middle). Sprinkle the top with cheese and stick it in the oven for exactly 8 minutes; it should be just set throughout.

  SERVES: 4 • ACTIVE PREPARATION TIME: 20 minutes • TOTAL PREPARATION TIME: ½ hour

slow-roasted tomato, basil & smoked mozzarella frittata

15g unsalted butter

1 tablespoon extra virgin olive oil

2 large shallots, peeled and thinly sliced

Coarse salt

Freshly ground black pepper

6 organic large eggs

125ml soya milk

6 halves (3 whole) Slow-Roasted Tomatoes (page 32), each cut in half

1 small ball (about 175g) lightly smoked mozzarella, torn into bite-sized pieces

2 fresh large basil leaves, roughly torn

Preheat the oven to 190°C (375°F) gas 5.

Heat the butter and olive oil over medium heat in a 25cm cast-iron frying pan. Sauté the shallots until soft and just barely browned, about 6 minutes. Season with plenty of salt and ground pepper.

Meanwhile, beat the eggs and soya milk in a mixing bowl. Pour over the shallots. Evenly distribute the tomatoes, cheese and basil. Let it cook for about 5 minutes, or until just set on the edges (it will still be very runny in the middle). Stick it in the oven for exactly 8 minutes; it should be just set throughout.

 SERVES: 4 • ACTIVE PREPARATION TIME: 20 minutes • TOTAL PREPARATION TIME: ½ hour

leek & gruyère frittata

15g unsalted butter

1 tablespoon extra virgin olive oil

1 large leek, washed and very thinly sliced

Coarse salt

Freshly ground black pepper

6 organic large eggs

125ml milk

50g Gruyère cheese, grated

Preheat the oven to 190°C (375°F) gas 5.

Heat the butter and olive oil over medium heat in a 25cm cast-iron frying pan. Sauté the leek slices until soft and just barely browned, 6–8 minutes. Season with plenty of salt and pepper.

Meanwhile, beat the eggs and milk to combine in a mixing bowl. Pour over the leek slices. Sprinkle the top with the cheese. Let it cook for about 5 minutes, or until just set on the edges (it will still be very runny in the middle). Stick it in the oven for exactly 8 minutes; it should be just set throughout.

 SERVES: 4 · **ACTIVE PREPARATION TIME: 20 minutes** · **TOTAL PREPARATION TIME: ½ hour**

morning pancakes

I ADD YOGURT TO THESE PANCAKES to give them a buttermilk-esque flavour (buttermilk has become hard to find in shops, especially in London). The Seed Mix adds flavour, texture and nutrients! My kids adore these and ask for them lots, especially my boy.

1	organic large egg
300ml	soya milk
5	tablespoons vegetable oil
125g	flour, your preference, any kind will work
1	teaspoon baking powder
3	tablespoons Seed Mix (page 222) (optional)
3	tablespoons natural yogurt
	Real Vermont maple syrup, for serving

Whisk the egg, soya milk, and 4 tablespoons vegetable oil together in a bowl. Stir in the flour, the baking powder, and the Seed Mix until just combined (overbeating is how you get tough pancakes). Fold in the yogurt. Heat a large non-stick frying pan or griddle over medium-high heat with 1 tablespoon of vegetable oil (or you could use butter . . . or if you use Jamie Oliver's unbelievable slippery non-stick cookware you don't need any fat). Ladle as many pancakes as possible onto your pan. Cook for about 2 minutes on the first side, or until the surface is covered with small bubbles and the underside is nicely browned. Flip and cook for about a minute on the second side. Remove the pancakes to a plate. Repeat the process until you run out of batter. Serve the pancakes stacked high with plenty of maple syrup.

 YIELD: about 2 dozen 7.5cm pancakes · **ACTIVE & TOTAL PREPARATION TIME:** 15–20 minutes

seed mix

THIS IS A FANTASTIC WAY to give yourself and your kids essential nutrients. Top porridge, granola, apple sauce (or anything!) for a crunchy texture and delicious flavour. You can also stir this mix into pancake, muffin or biscuit mixtures. Keep it in a jar in the refrigerator – it lasts for weeks.

1 part each pumpkin and sunflower seeds

2 parts each almonds, goji berries and flaxseeds

Finely grind everything together in a mini food processor or coffee grinder in batches if necessary.

YIELD: flexible · ACTIVE & TOTAL PREPARATION TIME: 5 minutes

home-made turkey sausage patties

I FIRST FEATURED THIS on my online newsletter GOOP for a holiday brunch menu. I wanted to create a healthy, organic sausage pattie that was not full of mystery meat, preservatives and the like. These have become a real breakfast favourite at our house, so I had to include them here.

1 teaspoon fennel seeds

Pinch crushed chillies

Pinch cayenne pepper

Pinch herbes de Provence salt (optional)

½ teaspoon coarse salt

¼ teaspoon freshly ground black pepper

1 teaspoon finely chopped fresh sage

225g minced turkey

2 teaspoons real Vermont maple syrup

2 tablespoons extra virgin olive oil

Using a pestle and mortar, a Flavour Shaker (gotta love Jamie Oliver) or mini food processor, bash the fennel seeds, crushed chillies, cayenne, salts and pepper together. Combine this spice mixture with the sage, turkey and maple syrup in a bowl until thoroughly combined.

Form the mixture into small, thin sausage-shaped patties. Heat the olive oil in a large non-stick pan over medium-high heat. Cook the sausages for about 1½ minutes on each side, pressing down with your spatula to really brown them and keep them thin. Serve warm.

make it kid friendly   You can make these without the chillies and cayenne for the kids.

 YIELD: 1 dozen small patties • ACTIVE & TOTAL PREPARATION TIME: 15 minutes

 You can even freeze the cooked patties and reheat them in the oven.

spiced apple crumb muffins

THESE NEXT TWO MUFFIN RECIPES are based on my friend Darlene's healthy recipes. D, as I call her, is a master at baking with alternative ingredients. The spelt flour has more nutritional value than regular wheat flour and it is easier to digest to boot. These are macrobiotic and super healthy, and my kids, as well as all visitors, gobble them up.

for the crumb topping

- 4 tablespoons white spelt flour
- 4 tablespoons whole spelt flour
- 4 tablespoons whole rolled oats (not instant and not steel-cut)
- 4 tablespoons unrefined dark brown sugar
- 2 teaspoons ground cinnamon
- Pinch sea salt
- 2 tablespoons vegetable oil
- 1 tablespoon soya milk

for the muffins

- 1 tablespoon cornflour
- 2 small apples peeled and finely diced
- 125ml vegetable oil, plus 2 tablespoons for greasing tin
- 150ml real Vermont maple syrup
- 150ml soya milk
- 100g white spelt flour
- 125g whole spelt flour
- 2¼ teaspoons baking powder
- ½ teaspoon bicarbonate of soda
- ¼ teaspoon fine salt
- 2 teaspoons ground cinnamon
- ½ teaspoon ground allspice
- 60g lightly toasted walnuts, roughly chopped

Preheat the oven to 180°C (350°F) gas 4. Line a 12-hole muffin tin with paper cases or oil it with 2 tablespoons of vegetable oil.

For the crumb topping, combine all the dry ingredients in a small bowl. Add the vegetable oil and soya milk and rub everything together with your fingers – the mixture should be lumpy. Set the mixture aside.

For the muffins, in a small bowl, toss the cornflour with the apples. In another large bowl, whisk together 125ml vegetable oil and all of the syrup and soya milk. Sift in the remaining ingredients (except for the walnuts) and fold in the apples and walnuts. Evenly distribute the batter in the muffin sections and bake for 25–30 minutes, or until a cocktail stick comes out clean.

YIELD: 1 dozen muffins • ACTIVE PREPARATION TIME: 15 minutes
TOTAL PREPARATION TIME: 45 minutes

banana walnut muffins

4	tablespoons plus 2 tablespoons rapeseed oil
125g	whole spelt flour
100g	white spelt flour
60g	barley flour
1	teaspoon bicarbonate of soda
1	teaspoon fine salt
3	very ripe medium bananas
125ml	real Vermont maple syrup
4	tablespoons brown rice syrup
1	tablespoon vanilla extract
85g	raisins
60g	toasted walnuts, chopped

Preheat the oven to 180°C (350°F) gas 4. Line a 12-hole muffin tin with paper cases or oil them with 2 tablespoons of rapeseed oil.

Sift the flours, bicarbonate of soda and salt into a medium-sized bowl. Purée the bananas in a food processor or blender and then add 4 tablespoons of rapeseed oil, syrups and vanilla and pulse to combine. Make a well in the flour mixture and pour in the liquid mixture. Stir just to combine and fold in the raisins and walnuts (don't overmix or you will have tough muffins!). Use an ice cream scoop to distribute the batter evenly among the muffin sections. Bake for approximately 25 minutes, or until a cocktail stick comes out clean. Cool in the pan for a few minutes before removing to a wire rack.

YIELD: 1 dozen muffins · ACTIVE PREPARATION TIME: 15 minutes
TOTAL PREPARATION TIME: 45 minutes

favourite granola

I LOVE CLASSIC GRANOLA as much as the next person and this version is pepped up with some Indian spice. It's got a bit of a kick to it.

200g	whole rolled oats (not instant and not steel-cut)
75g	whole unblanched almonds
4	tablespoons pumpkin seeds
4	tablespoons sunflower seeds
½	teaspoon garam masala
¼	teaspoon ground cinnamon
¼	teaspoon fine salt
125ml	real Vermont maple syrup
3	tablespoons light agave nectar or brown rice syrup
2	tablespoons vegetable oil
75g	dried cranberries, roughly chopped

Preheat the oven to 180°C (350°F) gas 4.

Stir together the oats, almonds, pumpkin and sunflower seeds, spices and salt in a large bowl. Combine the maple syrup, agave and vegetable oil in a small bowl and then mix with the dry ingredients. Spread the granola out on a non-stick baking tray or a regular baking tray covered with baking paper and coat with a little vegetable oil. Bake for 15–20 minutes, stirring occasionally, or until evenly browned. If you like your granola in clumps, remove the tray from the oven and push the granola so it's about 8mm thick, letting it cool completely and then breaking it apart into small pieces. If you like your granola loose, simply spread it out in the baking tray and let it cool. Either way, combine the cooled granola with the cranberries. It keeps well for 2–3 months in an airtight container.

 YIELD: about 450g • ACTIVE PREPARATION TIME: 10 minutes
TOTAL PREPARATION TIME: ½ hour plus cooling

blythe's blueberry muffins

THE BEST EVER. I GREW UP eating my mother's perfect blueberry muffins – they set an unbeatable standard – just the right balance of tart and sweet. When I was pregnant with my daughter, I asked my mother to make them for me all the time.

125g	unsalted butter, melted and cooled
2	organic large eggs
125ml	milk
225g	unbleached plain flour
175g	plus 1 teaspoon granulated sugar
2	teaspoons baking powder
½	teaspoon fine salt
300g	fresh blueberries

Preheat the oven to 190°C (375°F) gas 5. Line a 12-hole muffin tin with paper cases.

Whisk the butter, eggs and milk together in a bowl. In another bowl, whisk together the flour, the 175g sugar, baking powder and salt. Stir the wet ingredients into the dry ingredients and fold in the blueberries. Divide between the paper cases and sprinkle with the remaining teaspoon of sugar. Bake until a cocktail stick comes out clean and the muffins are golden brown, 25–30 minutes. Best to eat these warm.

YIELD: 1 dozen muffins • ACTIVE PREPARATION TIME: 15 minutes
TOTAL PREPARATION TIME: 45 minutes

healthier version of the blueberry muffins

THESE MUFFINS MADE FROM SPELT flour don't have any sugar and are vegan. They still rock the house.

125ml vegetable oil

125ml soya milk

125ml real Vermont maple syrup

4 tablespoons light agave nectar

100g white spelt flour

125g whole spelt flour

2 teaspoons baking powder

½ teaspoon fine salt

300g fresh blueberries

Preheat the oven to 190°C (375°F) gas 5. Line a 12-hole muffin tin with paper cases.

Mix wet ingredients together, stir in the dry ingredients and fold in the blueberries. Divide between the paper cases and bake until a cocktail stick comes out clean and the muffins are golden brown, 25–30 minutes. Let cool before eating (if you can. . .).

 YIELD: 1 dozen muffins • **ACTIVE PREPARATION TIME:** 15 minutes
TOTAL PREPARATION TIME: 45 minutes

challah french toast

MY BREAKFAST SPECIALITY. My family has asked me to make this at all hours of the day . . . and night. The challah bread is the perfect texture and flavour for French toast – it's unbeatable in my opinion.

1	vanilla pod or 1 teaspoon vanilla extract (use the pod to make Vanilla Sugar, page 31)
2	organic large eggs
250ml	milk
8	2cm-thick slices challah bread or brioche
25g	unsalted butter
1	teaspoon granulated sugar
1	banana, peeled
	Icing sugar, for serving
	Real Vermont maple syrup, for serving

Slice the vanilla pod in half lengthways. Use the tip of a paring knife to scrape out all of the seeds. Place the seeds in a bowl with a teaspoon of hot water and mix. Then crack the eggs into the bowl and whisk to blend, breaking up the sticky vanilla seeds. Whisk the milk in. Dip the bread into the egg mixture, coating each slice on both sides.

Meanwhile, melt the butter in a large frying pan over medium-high heat and add as many pieces of challah as can fit comfortably. Sprinkle the top of each piece with a tiny bit of granulated sugar. Cook for about 2 minutes, or until the underside is golden brown and the coating is crisp and lacy. Flip and sprinkle the cooked sides with a tiny bit of granulated sugar. Cook for about a minute or 2 longer, or until the second side is browned. Remove the French toast to a dish and repeat the process until all the pieces are cooked. Thinly slice the banana over the French toast, dust everything with icing sugar and serve with lots and lots of maple syrup.

 SERVES: 4 · **ACTIVE & TOTAL PREPARATION TIME: 15 minutes**

savoury rice bowl

NOW WE'RE TALKING. I LOVE a savoury breakfast – and this is right up my alley. I first had a version of this at a Japanese monastery during a silent retreat – don't ask, it's a long story. Anyway it was a great (interesting) experience but the savoury rice bowl was the best part. I came home and re-created it.

200g	short-grain brown rice
1.5l	water
	Soy sauce, for serving
	Toasted sesame oil, for serving
	Sesame and seaweed rice condiment (available at Japanese grocery shops), for serving
	Finely chopped spring onions, for serving
	Finely chopped kimchi, for serving
	Finely shredded nori, for serving

Rinse off the rice and combine with 1.25 litres of the water in a saucepan. Bring to the boil, turn the heat as low as it can go, cover, and cook for 1½ hours. The rice should be very soft. Add the remaining 250ml of water and cook for an additional 15–30 minutes. The mixture should be porridge-like.

To serve, spoon the rice into four bowls and top with the remaining ingredients, to suit your taste.

SERVES: 4 • ACTIVE PREPARATION TIME: 5 minutes • TOTAL PREPARATION TIME: 2 hours

OPPOSITE: Savoury Rice Bowl (top),
Sweet Rice Bowl (bottom)

sweet rice bowl

I LOVE THIS WARM, dreamy maple syrup-drenched rice porridge.
Sometimes when I'm pressed for time I just heat up some leftover brown rice
from the fridge with a bit of rice milk and top it the same way. A wonderful
wholesome way to start the day.

200ml short-grain brown rice

1.5l water

50g almonds for serving
(I like them whole and
raw, but roasted and
chopped is pretty great
too.)

Real Vermont maple
syrup, for serving

Rinse off the rice and combine with 1.25 litres of the water in a saucepan.
Bring to the boil, turn the heat as low as it can go, cover and cook for
1½ hours. The rice should be very soft. Add the remaining 250ml of
water and cook for an additional 15–30 minutes. The mixture should be
porridge-like.

To serve, spoon the rice into four bowls and top with the almonds and
as much maple syrup as you like.

SERVES: 4 • ACTIVE PREPARATION TIME: 5 minutes • TOTAL PREPARATION TIME: 2 hours

porridge

A PIPING HOT BOWL of oats can be so right in the morning, especially
topped with pure Vermont maple syrup, some berries or my healthy seed mix
– or whatever toppings you love. Instead of making it with full-fat milk,
I use soya milk, almond milk, rice milk or water (depending on the customer).

100g whole rolled oats
(not instant and not
steel-cut)

750ml water, soya, almond,
rice or regular milk

Small pinch salt

Blueberries,
blackberries, sliced
bananas, almonds,
raisins, maple syrup,
flaxseeds and/or Seed
Mix (page 222) –
whatever toppings
you love

Combine the oats, water and salt in a saucepan and set over medium heat.
Bring to a simmer and cook, stirring, for 5–7 minutes, or until desired
consistency is achieved. Serve with your favourite topping or combination
of toppings.

SERVES: 4 • ACTIVE & TOTAL PREPARATION TIME: 10 minutes

This is vegan if soya, almond or rice milk is used in place of regular milk.

bruce paltrow's world-famous pancakes

NOW IF THERE IS ONE IMAGE of my father that is the most 'him' – that is to say encapsulates all of his elements and delivers them in one picture – it would be him over his cast-iron griddles making his world-famous pancakes. These things have been legendary in our house for decades. He first got the recipe out of the *Joy of Cooking* and adapted it over the years to utter perfection. The recipe below is so truthful to his pancakes that it's almost hard for me to eat them, I keep expecting him to walk into the kitchen.

350g	unbleached plain flour
75g	granulated sugar
3½	teaspoons baking powder
2	teaspoons fine salt
750ml	buttermilk
75g	unsalted butter, melted and cooled, plus more butter for cooking
6	organic large eggs
	Up to 250ml milk, as needed to thin batter
	Real Vermont maple syrup, warmed, for serving

Whisk the dry ingredients together in a large bowl. Whisk the buttermilk, butter and eggs together in another bowl. Add the wet ingredients to the dry ingredients, whisking just enough to combine (small lumps are okay). Let the batter sit, covered, overnight. The next morning, heat up your griddle or favourite non-stick pan and slick it with a little butter. Add enough milk to the batter to thin it to the right consistency – the thicker the batter, the thicker and heavier your pancakes; the thinner the batter, the more delicate your pancakes – neither is wrong. Cook the pancakes on the griddle, flipping them after bubbles appear on the surface of the uncooked side. Let cook 2–3 minutes more, then remove and eat with lots of warm maple syrup.

 YIELD: 3 dozen 12.5cm pancakes • ACTIVE PREPARATION TIME: 20 minutes
TOTAL PREPARATION TIME: 20 minutes plus overnight resting

blythe's savoury bread pudding

MY MOM USED TO MAKE THIS when company would come for an elegant, relaxed brunch. As this could be prepared before the doorbell rang, she could set everything up and enjoy herself once the guests arrived. It's very rich, so it's not great for an everyday breakfast. It's best to cut the richness with a Buck's fizz...

200g	1cm bread cubes (I use a 30cm-long loaf of soft French bread with the crusts removed.)
2	tablespoons extra virgin olive oil
	Coarse salt
4	organic large eggs
175ml	double cream
2	teaspoons fresh thyme leaves, finely chopped
¼	teaspoon freshly ground black pepper
	A little butter for the pan
50g	mature Cheddar cheese, grated

Preheat the oven to 190°C (375°F) gas 5.

Spread the bread cubes out on a baking sheet, drizzle evenly with the olive oil and sprinkle with a large pinch of salt. Bake for 7–8 minutes, stirring halfway through, or until lightly browned and crispy.

While the bread cubes are cooling, whisk together the eggs, cream, thyme, pepper and a pinch of salt. Stir the bread cubes into the custard mixture and let it sit for at least 10 minutes (up to overnight).

Turn the oven down to 180°C (350°F) gas 4.

Pour the mixture into a buttered 23cm cake tin or 20cm square tin (or divide it evenly between individual ramekins). Sprinkle the cheese on top and bake for 20 minutes, or until the cheese is bubbling and lightly browned. Serve warm.

SERVES: 4–6 • ACTIVE PREPARATION TIME: 25 minutes
TOTAL PREPARATION TIME: at least 45 minutes

This can be made ahead up to the point of baking.

scrambled eggs
with smoked salmon
& cream cheese

THIS IS A GREAT BREAKFAST dish when you are feeding a group.
You can always leave out the salmon for the kids, but they love the cream
cheese and chives.

8	organic large eggs
	Splash milk
	Big pinch coarse salt
	A few grinds black pepper
	Big knob unsalted butter
150g	smoked salmon, torn into bite-sized pieces
80g	cream cheese
2	teaspoons finely sliced fresh chives, for serving

Whisk the eggs together with the milk, salt and pepper. Melt the butter in a large non-stick frying pan over medium heat. Add the eggs, let them sit for 1 minute, turn the heat to medium-low and push them gently with a wooden spoon for 1½ minutes, or until very soft curds form. Fold in the salmon, dot with the cream cheese, turn the heat as low as it can go and cover the pan for 1½ minutes, or until the cheese begins to get oozy. Sprinkle with chives and serve.

 SERVES: 4 · ACTIVE & TOTAL PREPARATION TIME: 10 minutes

omelette

A FLUFFY, DINER-STYLE OMELETTE that can be dressed up however you like to please any member of the family.

15g unsalted butter

3 organic large eggs, very well beaten

Coarse salt

Freshly ground black pepper

Whatever filling you like (grated cheese, cooked mushrooms, Slow-Roasted Tomatoes, page 32, etc.)

Heat the butter in a small non-stick frying pan (15–18cm in diameter) over medium heat. Add the eggs and season the top with a pinch of salt and a grind of pepper. Cover the pan with a dinner plate and let them cook for 30 seconds. If you'd like to fill your omelette, at this point remove the plate and sprinkle over your desired filling, put the plate back on top and cook for 30 more seconds. Take off the plate (incidentally, you now have a warm plate that will be perfect for the almost finished omelette) and tilt the pan side to side to make sure the eggs are evenly cooked. Cook for about 30 seconds more and then slip a flexible spatula under half of the omelette and carefully fold it over the other half as if closing a book. Pat the omelette down, cook for 1 minute, and then flip the entire thing over with the spatula and cook for another 30–60 seconds. Remove the omelette from the pan onto your warm plate, sprinkle with a tiny bit more salt and an extra grating of cheese if you like. This makes an omelette that's browned on the outside, but if you prefer something more gentle, simply turn the heat down a notch.

SERVES: 1 • **ACTIVE & TOTAL PREPARATION TIME: 5 minutes**

desserts

I came across an axiom in a passage from a culinary memoir called *Heat* in which the author, Bill Buford, observes the following: 'You can divide people into two categories in life: cooks and bakers.' I am definitely in the former category. In my mind, baking pastries, biscuits, cakes and the like is scientific – it allows for little improv. Some of my desserts require some baking but more of them are a bit more free-form and have room for adjustment to your personal taste. For me a dash of home-made hot fudge sauce, a banana and some roasted nuts over ice cream just hits the spot. More often than not when I prepare desserts, I am thinking about keeping the sugar intake low, as well as limiting other ingredients that don't do us any favours. I don't want to overload my kids with sugar seven days a week. With that in mind, many of these recipes, while tasting very decadent, are actually full of healthier ingredients.
A cool trick that healthy baker Darlene Gross taught me.

fudgy chocolate brownies

THESE ARE ABOUT AS HEALTHY as brownies can get, with no flavour sacrifice.

200g	white spelt flour
100g	high-quality cocoa powder
1½	tablespoons baking powder
	Pinch fine salt
125ml	vegetable oil
250ml	real Vermont maple syrup
125ml	brown rice syrup or light agave nectar
125ml	strong brewed coffee
125ml	soya milk
1	tablespoon vanilla extract
175g	high-quality chocolate chips (try and find the grain-sweetened variety if you want to stay sugar free)

Preheat the oven to 180°C (350°F) gas 4. Grease a baking dish (I use a 28 x 23cm dish that's 5cm deep) with vegetable oil.

Sift the flour, cocoa, baking powder and salt together in a large mixing bowl. In a separate bowl, whisk together the vegetable oil, syrups, coffee, soya milk and vanilla. Mix the wet ingredients into the dry ingredients, being careful not to overbeat (that's how you end up with tough cake!). Pour half the mixture into the baking dish. Sprinkle with half the chocolate chips. Pour the rest of the mixture into the baking dish and sprinkle with the rest of the chocolate chips. Bake for 30 minutes (less if your dish is shallow, more if it's deep), or until a cocktail stick has just a bit of chocolate on it when you test the cake (this means it'll be super fudgy!). Let it cool if you have patience, cut into squares and serve.

SERVES: about 8 • **ACTIVE PREPARATION TIME:** 15 minutes
TOTAL PREPARATION TIME: 45 minutes

grandad danner's favourite peanut butter cookies

BASED ON MY GRANDMOTHER'S very old recipe, these cookies are a slightly softer version of my grandad Danner's favourite peanut butter cookies. These were his favourite things on earth and my grandmother always made them for him. He passed away when I was seven, but I can still remember him with his thick shock of white hair eating these cookies with a glass of milk.

150g	unbleached plain flour
½	teaspoon bicarbonate of soda
½	teaspoon baking powder
½	teaspoon fine salt
125g	unsalted butter, at room temperature
175g	smooth peanut butter, at room temperature
125g	dark brown sugar
125g	light brown sugar
1	organic large egg, at room temperature
1	teaspoon vanilla extract
175g	peanut butter chips (available at Panzers, London, and other specialist delis)
50g	granulated sugar (optional)

Preheat oven to 180°C (350°F) gas 4.

Whisk together the dry ingredients in a medium bowl. In a large bowl, cream together the butter, peanut butter and brown sugars. Stir in the egg and vanilla. Add the flour in thirds and stir until smooth. Fold in the peanut butter chips. Roll the mixture into golf-ball-sized balls (about 1½ tablespoons). At this point you can roll them in granulated sugar or you can press each cookie down with the tines of a fork. Either way, bake for 10 minutes, in a non-stick baking tray, rotating the tray halfway through baking time. Cool the cookies on a rack before serving.

 YIELD: about 30 cookies • ACTIVE PREPARATION TIME: 10 minutes
TOTAL PREPARATION TIME: 20 minutes

oatmeal raisin cookies

THESE ARE MY ABSOLUTE FAVOURITE healthy treat. They are so guilt free they can hardly be called cookies, except they taste delicious.

75g	raisins
90g	toasted walnuts
100g	whole rolled oats (not instant and not steel-cut)
50g	white spelt flour
90g	whole spelt flour
1½	teaspoons ground cinnamon
1	teaspoon bicarbonate of soda
½	teaspoon fine salt
5	tablespoons vegetable oil
5	tablespoons real Vermont maple syrup
5	tablespoons brown rice syrup
2	teaspoons vanilla extract

Preheat the oven to 180°C (350°F) gas 4. Line baking sheets with baking paper.

Place the raisins in a small bowl and cover with boiling water to plump them.

Meanwhile, finely grind the walnuts and half the oats in a small food processor. Combine this mixture with the remaining dry ingredients in a large mixing bowl. Mix together the wet ingredients in a small bowl and add to the dry-ingredients bowl. Stir to combine. Drain the raisins and fold them into the mixture. Drop large spoonfuls of the mixture onto the baking sheets. Bake for 13–15 minutes until browned. Remove to a wire rack.

YIELD: about 18 cookies • **ACTIVE PREPARATION TIME:** 15 minutes
TOTAL PREPARATION TIME: ½ hour

'I don't have a sweet tooth. *All* my teeth are sweet.'
—MOSES

home-made root beer floats

WHEN I WAS GROWING UP, my dad used to take me to the A&W drive-in for hot dogs and his favourite sweet dessert refreshment on earth, the root beer float. My dad was a root beer man and drilled into me the fine attributes of the drink early in life. It's only when I grew up and read the side of the can that I became disillusioned about enjoying it regularly. I wondered how difficult it would be to make my own organic version, devoid of colouring. As it turned out, not difficult at all. The day we were finding the formula, my daughter, who was four years old at the time, walked into the kitchen and asked me what I was drinking. 'Soda,' I replied. She looked at me with her big blue eyes. 'What's that?' she responded. With this version, I felt good about letting her discover it for herself.

500ml	water
2	cloves
8	peppercorns
4	tablespoons sassafras extract
50g	unrefined dark brown sugar
	5cm piece fresh ginger, peeled and crushed with the back of your knife
	Soda water
4	scoops vanilla ice cream

Combine the water, cloves, peppercorns, sassafras, sugar and ginger together in a small saucepan. Bring to the boil, lower the heat and simmer until a nice syrup forms, about 10 minutes. Let the syrup cool, strain out the solids, and then divide it between four small glasses. Dilute it with soda water so the drink reaches your desired strength (I like about 150ml).

Drop a scoop of ice cream into each glass. Heaven.

note: Sassafras extract is essential for making this great American classic but I don't think it's available yet outside of the US. I get mine from Flower Power Herbs & Roots, (a funky store in NYC's East Village, and you can order it online at flowerpower.net).

SERVES: 4 • **ACTIVE PREPARATION TIME:** 10 minutes
TOTAL PREPARATION TIME: 15 minutes plus cooling

lalo's famous cookies

LALO (AS MY MOTHER is affectionately called by my children – who wants to be called Grandma anyway?) is famous far and wide for these delicious cookies. They are incredibly good for you – I even let my kids have them with breakfast – not a bad ingredient in the bunch. I use a non-stick baking sheet for baking.

450g	barley flour
450g	unblanched whole almonds, crushed in a food processor (about ten 2-second pulses)
1	teaspoon fine salt
1	teaspoon ground cinnamon
250ml	rapeseed oil
250ml	real Vermont maple syrup
	Your favourite jam (blueberry, raspberry and apricot are all very nice)

Preheat the oven to 180°C (350°F) gas 4.

Combine all the ingredients except for the jam together in a large bowl with a wooden spoon. Form tablespoonfuls into balls and space them evenly on baking sheets. Using your index finger, make an indent in each cookie. Fill each indent with a small spoonful of jam. Bake until cookies are evenly browned, about 20 minutes. Let cool before eating.

YIELD: about 50 cookies · ACTIVE PREPARATION TIME: 25 minutes
TOTAL PREPARATION TIME: 45 minutes

pomegranate granita

GRANITA IS AN EASY WAY to have a lovely, healthy, refreshing dessert. I like
this one – Granita Granada as I like to call it (*granada* means 'pomegranate' in
Spanish). No sugar, no dairy, all goodness.

500ml fresh pomegranate
juice

  1 tablespoon fresh
lemon juice

  4 tablespoons light
agave nectar

  4 tablespoons fresh
pomegranate seeds

Whisk together the juices and agave and pour into a 20cm metallic pie dish
or another similar-sized container. Freeze for 1 hour. Take out of the freezer
and scrape with a fork. Repeat this process every 15 minutes for the next
2 hours. You should end up with a solid mixture that resembles flakes of
sorbet. Alternatively, you can freeze it overnight and scrape it before serving.
To serve, scoop into six glasses or bowls and sprinkle with the fresh
pomegranate seeds.

note: To get the most flavour and brilliant colour, only use 100 per cent
pomegranate juice from the refrigerated section of the supermarket.

 SERVES: 6 • ACTIVE PREPARATION TIME: 15 minutes • TOTAL PREPARATION TIME: 3 hours

margarita granita

NOT A GRANITA FOR THE KIDDIES — this is a fun dessert for a grown-up
dinner party or as an aperitif in a little cup on a summer night.

Zest of 1 lime

125ml fresh lime juice
(4–5 medium limes)

4 tablespoons light
agave nectar

250ml water

4 tablespoons highest-
quality tequila

Whisk everything together and pour into a 20cm metallic pie dish or another
similar-sized container. Freeze for 1 hour. Take out of the freezer and scrape
with a fork. Repeat this process every 15 minutes for the next 2 hours.
You should end up with a solid mixture that resembles flakes of sorbet.
Alternatively, you can freeze it overnight and scrape it before serving.
To serve, scoop into six glasses (salt the rims if you like).

SERVES: 6 • **ACTIVE PREPARATION TIME:** 15 minutes • **TOTAL PREPARATION TIME:** 3 hours

mutti's pecan butterballs

MY GRANDMOTHER MUTTI WAS – how shall I say this? – a unique person. She shone when she was entertaining – cooking, singing, baking. These butterballs were the big treat in our house at Christmastime. Mutti would lovingly make and roll the balls and they would disappear. Careful not to inhale the icing sugar!

225g	unsalted butter, at room temperature
225g	pecans, finely chopped or pulsed in a food processor
300g	unbleached plain flour
	Pinch fine salt
50g	plus 2 tablespoons icing sugar

Preheat oven to 180°C (350°F) gas 4.

Mix everything, except the 50g sugar together in a mixing bowl with your hands. Roll tablespoonfuls into balls and place on 2 non-stick baking sheets. Bake for 20 minutes, rotating the sheets halfway through baking. When they're nearly cool, gently roll each ball in the 50g sugar. Put the leftover sugar in a sieve and shake over the cookies. These keep well in a tin, for a week.

YIELD: about 50 cookies · ACTIVE PREPARATION TIME: 25 minutes
TOTAL PREPARATION TIME: 45 minutes

blueberry pavlova

PAVLOVA IS EASY AND KIND of foolproof. Just use fresh ripe blueberries,
or any kind you like really – it's so delicious with meringue. I like to make this
after I make home-made pasta so I don't waste the egg whites.

4	organic large egg whites
	Pinch fine salt
½	teaspoon white vinegar
175g	plus 2 tablespoons granulated sugar
1	tablespoon cornflour
½	teaspoon vanilla extract
250ml	double cream
175g	fresh blueberries, plus more for serving

Preheat the oven to 180°C (350°F) gas 4.

Combine egg whites, salt and white vinegar together in the bowl of an electric mixer and beat on high speed until soft peaks form. Combine the 175g of sugar and cornflour together in a small bowl and add to the egg whites in thirds, whisking each addition in completely. Add the vanilla and beat until stiff peaks form.

Line a baking tray with baking paper and spoon the meringue in 8 big spoonfuls, using a spoon to spread each in a circle, and then make an indent in each. Bake for 10 minutes, lower the heat to 110°C (200°F) gas ¼, and bake for another hour. Turn off the heat and cool the meringues in the oven for an hour, propping the door open with a wooden spoon.

Meanwhile, whip the cream together with the remaining 2 tablespoons of sugar. In a small bowl, crush 50g of the blueberries with a potato masher or a spoon to release their juice. Fold those and the rest of the blueberries into the cream if you like, or use as a topping over the egg whites and cream. Evenly distribute the cream on the meringues, filling in the indentations. Top with juicy blueberries and serve.

SERVES: 8 • **ACTIVE PREPARATION TIME: 15 minutes** • **TOTAL PREPARATION TIME: 2½ hours**

berries with caramelized cream

ONE EVENING WHEN I HAD my wood-burning stove going
I realized I hadn't thought of dessert. I found some frozen berries in the
freezer and since I didn't have time to make a cobbler, I whipped up a sweet
cream topping for the berries and whacked them in the oven. The cream
topping went all lovely and brown and the whole thing was made and done in
about seven minutes.

500g	blueberries, blackberries and/or raspberries
2	tablespoons sour cream
2	tablespoons double cream
1	organic large egg
1	organic egg white
250g	mascarpone
3	tablespoons icing sugar
	Pinch fine sea salt
	Seeds of 1 vanilla pod (use the scraped pod for your Vanilla Sugar, page 31)

Preheat the grill and put the oven shelf in the middle or lower half of your
grill compartment.

Put the berries in a pie or casserole dish. Whisk together the remaining
ingredients until completely smooth and pour over the berries. Put the dish
under the grill and cook just until the topping is browned and caramelized,
5–10 minutes.

SERVES: 6 • ACTIVE & TOTAL PREPARATION TIME: 10 minutes

This can be made ahead up to the point of grilling.

seasonal crumble

ONE OF MY ABSOLUTE FAVOURITE things to do with my children is to pick fruit for crumble, a dessert we love. We never seem to have enough of any one berry all at the same time, so we either do mixed berries or peaches in the summer, and apple in the autumn. This is a fantastic thing to do if you can pick fruit somewhere and have your kids participate in the whole process. From washing the fruit to mixing and assembling, they can actually make the whole thing virtually by themselves. They will really get a sense of where everything comes from and the steps we take to turn it into something delicious. This recipe utilizes the sweetness of the fruit, cutting down on added sugar, always a good thing.

500g	fruit (sliced peaches, diced apples, blackberries, blueberries, etc.)
5	tablespoons white spelt flour
100g	whole rolled oats (not instant and not steel-cut)
50g	unrefined dark brown sugar
¼	teaspoon ground cinnamon
	Pinch fine salt
50g	unsalted butter, at room temperature
	Ice cream, for serving

Preheat the oven to 180°C (350°F) gas 4.

Combine the fruit with 1 tablespoon of flour in a 23cm pie dish or similar-sized baking dish. Combine the rest of the ingredients (except the ice cream) together in a mixing bowl, using your hands to form pea-sized crumbs. Sprinkle the topping evenly over the fruit. Bake for 45 minutes, or until the topping is browned and the fruit juices are bubbling. Serve warm with ice cream.

SERVES: 6 · ACTIVE PREPARATION TIME: 15 minutes · TOTAL PREPARATION TIME: 1 hour

This can be made ahead up until the point of baking.

my favourite home-made hot fudge sauce

BROWN RICE SYRUP, THOUGH LESS COMMON than golden syrup, is worth seeking out because it lends the fudge a rounder, smoother, less saccharine flavour and it's also a lot better for you. If you can't find it, golden syrup is totally OK to use and I've even found organic varieties. This is perfect over ice cream or as a dip for fruit, especially good with strawberries and bananas.

75g dark chocolate (62 per cent cocoa solids), finely chopped

4 tablespoons double cream

2 tablespoons brown rice syrup (or golden syrup)

Combine all of the ingredients in a double boiler (or in a metal or glass bowl set above a small pan of simmering water) and stir until completely melted, about 3 minutes. Serve warm.

 SERVES: 4 · **ACTIVE & TOTAL PREPARATION TIME: 5 minutes**

RELIABLE ONLINE
RESOURCES

I've tailored this list for the UK. You can find most things via the wonder of the web now, but these sites are the go-to places I rely on:

Borough Market, London for everything!

brindisa.com/store for everything Spanish

coolchile.co.uk for Mexican ingredients: chillies, tortillas, chipotle, etc.

japancentre.com for Asian ingredients

panzers.co.uk for harder-to-find American foods

planetorganic.com for gluten-free baking mix, egg-free mayo, etc.

spicesofindia.co.uk for every spice you could imagine!

wholefoodsmarket.com for all things natural and organic

acknowledgements

I am indebted to the lovely and inspirational Ellen Silverman for her beautiful photos, Susie Theodorou for the food styling and good humour, Sara Slavin for the prop styling, and everyone else who helped make the photo production a reality: Nick Duers, Rebecca Jurkevich, Kristin Knauff, Amy Neunsinger and family, Loren Simpson, Leslie Lopez, Adir Abergel, Ashlie Johnson, and Meyler & Company. And for the cover shoot: Lucy Attwater, Renato Campora, Kristofer Buckle, Kevin Norris and, of course, Ellen.

Additional gratitude to Harold Brown, Luke Janklow, Dani Wells-Cole and the truly amazing Cleo Brock-Abraham. And to Stephen Huvane for twenty years of support.

Karen Murgolo and the team at Grand Central Publishing, including Matthew Ballast, Philippa White, Tareth Mitch, Anne Twomey and Claire Brown. And to Laura Palese, for a beautiful design.

And of course. . .Georgie, Eliza, Kevin, Elouisa, Reina, Ljube, Victoria and Julio, Aimee, Marta, Laura, Leticia and the wonderful Terry Abbot.

I tip my hat to the chefs, home cooks, food authors and restaurateurs who have been my teachers. . .starting with my dear friend and professor of all things, Mario Batali. The chef friends of my parents who opened up the culinary world to us Paltrows – the late Sheila Lukins, one of my mother's closest friends, for her wonderful eccentricity in the kitchen and out; Michael and Kim McCarty, our conduit to the food revolution in California; Jonathan Waxman; and Gordon Naccarato. Lee and Darlene Gross, who taught me more than anyone about healthy eating; Jamie Oliver, for one of the best cooking lessons imaginable. Arjun Waney for his incredible kitchens and friendship. The Elio's kitchen, the Chez L'Ami Louis kitchen and of course the inimitable Ruthie Rogers and the River Cafe kitchen.

credits Sue Fisher King (San Francisco), D'Artagnan, TableArt (Los Angeles), Unici (West Hollywood), Rina Menardi (Los Angeles)

index

about the author

Gwyneth Paltrow is an Oscar-winning actress, founder of GOOP.com, co-author with Mario Batali of *Spain, A Culinary Road Trip* and mother of two. She splits her time between London and New York.